Stuff They Didn't Teach You in School

BY BRIAN HIGHLEY

A

ABC

'Go!' is the shortest complete sentence in English.

The two most commonly used words in the English language are 'I' and 'you'.

'Set' has the highest number of definitions with 484 in the 'Oxford English Dictionary'. 'Run' runs a distant second with 396.

It is claimed that 11% of everything ever written in the English language consists of the letter E.

The above sentence consists of 78 letters, 2 numbers and a symbol (by my count). I don't think this is 11% of Es but I was rubbish in maths at school.

Over 80% of information stored on computers across the world is in English.

In 2011 'lol' was added as a word to the 'Oxford Dictionary'. In 2012 an online survey revealed that 85% of under-25s using social networking realise that 'lol' stands for 'laughing out loud'. 46% of over-45s used 'lol' for 'lots of love', causing much offence when someone reports a death in the family and receives the reply 'lol.' (See Foreign Phrases)

Mackintosh raincoats are made from a waterproof fabric invented by Charles Macintosh.

Nobody has ever given an acceptable explanation why something is called a Mackintosh when it was invented by a Macintosh.

The English language has 44 distinct sounds and there are 1,100 different ways of spelling these.

You can spell every number from one to 99 without using any of the letters A, B, C or D.

The sentence 'He believed Caesar could see people seizing the seas,' includes all seven ways of spelling 'ee' in the English language.

AFTERNOON T/V

Afternoon television programmes demand one common element, they must be extremely cheap to produce.

Unknown actors ham their way around hospital wards and police stations. Out of work, not at all funny, comedians host quiz shows. Chefs are allowed to shamelessly plug their restaurants in exchange for sharing a few recipes with amateur cooks.

Anyone who lives within a few miles of the coast will remember when monkfish, if not being breadcrumbed to masquerade as scampi, were either thrown back into the water or used as bait. Then TV chefs got hold of the stuff and it became one of the most expensive items on the fishmonger's slab.

Mackerel fling themselves on to the nearest hook, amateur fishermen give them away and they're fine to eat if tossed on to a barbecue while still stiff and shiny-eyed. TV chefs have now started worshiping mackerel so it won't be long before their price rockets and they appear in trendy eateries at the same price as lobster.

Lamb once had to be rare, now it has to be slow-cooked for six hours. No matter what your mother told you about the multiple illnesses caused by undercooked pork, pork is now perfect if pink.

Most prolific among afternoon TV programmes are the so called 'antique' shows. Like chefs plugging their restaurants, auctioneers take it in turns to advertise each other's sale rooms by selling-on junk purchased at car boot sales.

Clarice Cliff and William Moorcroft are so commonly recognisable following ceaseless TV exposure that they even creep into questions aimed at pensioners and unemployable dog toenail technicians on afternoon quiz shows. Yet works by these two pottery decorators still regularly turn up for a few pence at car boots frequented by TV antique experts.

Diecast toy cars that used to be as common as free mackerel are worth a fortune so long as they're still in the box. What boy was ever given a shiny 007 Maserati and kept the box?

Then there are those who scrawl the 'autographs' of the Fab Four on the sleeve of their Sgt Pepper CD (See Beatles) and flog this on an afternoon show for a four-figure sum. John Lennon died in 1980 and the first rock CD was Billy Joel's '52nd Street', released in 1982, but this doesn't seem to matter to our experts.

It is truly amazing how many people are 'downsizing'.

'Why are you selling your grandmother's wedding ring?'

'We are downsizing.'

The expert always fails to ask the obvious follow-up question. 'So how much space does this wedding ring take up?'

There are several antique shows that conveniently ignore the seller's and buyer's premiums. Today's happy, smiling auctioneer, who was probably on yesterday's show in the capacity of buyer or contestant adviser, not only gets free advertising on the BBC, plus fee and expenses, but everything going through his auction room attracts two fees. So if the hammer falls at £100 for grandma's wedding ring the average friendly gavel basher will collect 15% + VAT from the seller and the same from the buyer.

All of the cookery shows conveniently ignore the chef's premium. The mackerel costing £1, or free if you live close to the sea, will have escalated in price by one thousand percent by the time one of the chef's lackeys has cut it into four tiny portions, pin-boned and pan fried it. Pan fried? I have never understood that menu term, what else are you going to fry it in if you don't fry it in a pan? Of course, even after pocketing the mark-up on his mackerel, the chef cannot afford to pay his kitchen workers or waiting staff a living wage which accounts for the 15% service charge added to your bill.

American afternoon TV is even worse than that in the U.K. Commercials for headache pills and cures for indigestion spend more time warning potential customers of the possible adverse affect than about the curative qualities of the product.

There's been little change in American TV since 1953 when the Communion Service during Elizabeth II's Coronation was interrupted by commercials for Pepperell's Sheets and a collection of General Motors' car badges called 'America's Crown Jewels'. Some of the serious bits of the age-old ceremony were fronted by J. Fred Muggs, a chimpanzee.

One final thought on afternoon TV. Why does that woman on

commercials for disabled/senior citizen bathtubs always wear a swimsuit in the bath? (See Bathrooms)

ALE AND HEARTY

Beer contains almost all the minerals required for human survival. When nutrition was poor in the Middle Ages beer was consumed for its nutritional values and because it was much safer than water from the public supplies.

Old Speckled Hen, the very popular ale, was originally brewed by the Morland Brewery in Abingdon, Oxfordshire, to celebrate the 50th anniversary of the nearby MG car factory.

Workers at the factory used an old MG as a runaround that became covered with spots of paint over the years. The vehicle was well known around the town where it was nicknamed the 'Owld Speckled Un,' (Old Speckled One). This was translated into 'Old Speckled Hen' by the brewery to make its name more accessible to beer drinkers who didn't know this story.

Cenosillicaphobia is the fear of an empty beer glass.

In 2005 a Slovak man was driving his Audi in the Tatra mountains when an avalanche buried him and his car. He attempted to dig himself out but snow came in through the window faster than he could clear it. He drank sixty bottles of beer, yes sixty, he had in the car and created a passage to freedom by urinating. Rescuers found him, staggering drunk on the mountain, four days after the avalanche.

Most beers, wines and juice products are clarified by the use of a product called finings. Finings usually includes gelatine, casein, albumen or, most commonly, isinglass which is made from the dried swim bladders of fish. This obviously makes such drinks unsuitable for vegetarians.

Hops used in brewing are from the same plant family as marijuana.

German beer was hallucinogenic until the addition of henbane was banned in 1516.

In the 19th century Munich mothers would drink up to seven pints of beer per day believing this was necessary in order to breast-feed.

For many years it was claimed that leeches fed on beer would suck more blood. Scientists at the University of Bergen tested the theory and also fed some leeches with garlic or soured cream. Each researcher placed a selection of leeches on their arms. The sour cream leeches showed increased sucking ability. The garlic-fed leeches dropped dead. As might be expected, the leeches that had been given beer swayed around and could not maintain their grip.

Young Inca girls were employed to chew corn into a pulp. They spat the pulp into vats of warm water where it festered for several weeks before being strained to become beer.

European children were baptised with beer, or sometimes cider, in the 13th century.

Recent reports by American scientists suggest what most regular pub-goers have known all along. Beer is good for you.

The New England Journal of Medicine announced that women who drink moderate quantities of beer have better cognitive functions than non-drinkers.

Researchers discovered that the alcohol in beer raises HDL cholesterol, that's the good cholesterol associated with a lower risk of heart disease.

The American Journal of Epidemiology reports that beer consumption can be inversely associated with the risk of kidney stones in middle-aged men. A bottle of beer per day is estimated to reduce risk by 40%.

ANIMAL HEROS

A ferret called Nipper pulled a chord through a pipe linking Buckingham Palace to the Victoria Memorial which was then used to pull through a heavy cable that was used for a large part of the TV coverage of Prince Charles' and Princes Diana's wedding.

In 1998 a four-year-old Merino sheep became international news after disappearing from a farm in New Zealand.

Shrek lived off the land for six years prior to being found sheltering in a cave. 75% of his body was covered by a thick coat of wool due to having avoided annual shearing.

An average Merino sheep fleece weights 9.9 pounds, Shrek's weighed in at an incredible 60 pounds, enough wool to make twenty men's suits. Shrek's shearing was broadcast live on national television and such was his celebrity he was taken to parliament to meet the Prime Minister. (See Little Lamb)

One of the most frequently heard pub quiz questions asks for the name of the dog who discovered the World Cup when it went missing in England prior to the World Cup Final. The well known answer is Pickles.

Few pub quizzers know the answer to the question; 'Which 1966 World Cup hero was strangled to death?' The answer is poor Pickles who got his lead caught around his neck while chasing a cat.

The largest known captive elephant was called Ziggy. Ziggy could play 'Yes Sir, That's My Baby', on the harmonica and he smoked cigarettes.

A German zoo dropped plans to house homosexual penguins in separate pens following complaints from a gay-rights group.

APOSTLE SPOONS

Apostle Spoons, spoons with saintly little figures on the end of their handles, regularly show up on TV antique shows (See Afternoon TV) and none of the experts ever question why they always come in sets of twelve. Every mention of apostles in religious books I have checked refer to their number as being twelve

When he popped into the pub for half a shandy I asked my local vicar how many apostles there were and he replied 'Is this a catch question? Obviously there were twelve.'

No it isn't a catch question. Matthias took over from Judas and Paul was a late addition. By my reckoning this makes a total of fourteen so sets of twelve apostle spoons are short-changing you by two spoons.

John was the only apostle to witness the crucifixion of Christ.

APPLES

Colnbrook is a village situated between the M4 and M25, close to Heathrow Airport. When this was an idyllic country hamlet in 1825 a brewer named Richard Cox grew the first Cox's Orange Pippin here.

Cox described his fruit as having, 'All characters so admirably blended and balanced to please the palate and nose as no other apple can do. The greatest apple of this age.'

To this day most connoisseurs recognise the Cox's Orange Pippin as by far the best fresh eating apple.

Apples are a member of the rose family.

'Moss Cider' is produced in Manchester's Moss Side.

At the start of 2015 there were 5,803 people in the USA with the surname Apple.

Apples ripen ten times faster out of the fridge.

Isaac Newton was reportedly hit on the head by a falling apple which gave him his theory for gravity. Newton actually confirmed this story although a witness said he only saw the apple fall from the branch to the ground without it actually landing on Newton's head. The incident took place in Cambridge and the variety of apple that inspired the scientist was almost certainly a large, green-skinned variety, Flower of Kent.

The science of apple growing is called pomology.

The only apple native to the USA is the crabapple.

A grapple is an apple that tastes like a grape.

Apple juice is sold as cider in Canada and the USA. What the British and Irish know as cider is called Hard Cider, or Applejack across the pond.

Teeth whitening products usually contain a stain dissolving chemical, malic acid, that is found in apples.

If you place an apple in a bag of potatoes it keeps the potatoes fresh and prevents sprouting.

APPROPRIATE NAMES

A name suited to its owner is an aptronym.

The 2003 World Poker Champion who won $2.5 million is called Chris Moneymaker.

In 1793 French gastronome Jean-Anthelme Brillat-Savarin became mayor of the town of Belly.

Sun Prairie Fire Department, Wisconsin, USA, employs a fire fighter called Les McBurney.

In 1833 a man called Jack Ferry crossed the English Channel on a floating bicycle.

In 1557 Robert Calf was trampled to death by a cow.

The director of the Centre for Social Justice who joined Theresa May's Downing Street team in 2017 is called Christian Guy.

A senior American Republican politician who served in the House of Representatives has the name Rich White.

In Leeds there is a law firm called Godloves Solicitors.

ARRESTING

In 1990 a wedding in Flint, Michigan, was attended by 15 leading drug pushers. Debra Williams, the bride, lifted her skirt for the traditional garter photograph but instead of showing her legs she produced a gun. Debbie was an undercover police officer. Many of the guests also pulled out guns, they were also undercover cops . The signal for the action to begin was when the band struck up with the song 'I Fought the Law.'

Phillip Joseph Smolinsky (36) was arrested in Florida for attacking his girlfriend with a banana. He was charged with domestic violence.

Bryan Paul Simpson was jailed for four and half years in Kansas after taking his neighbour's pet spider hostage in 2012.

In 2007 the police in Iran arrested 14 squirrels on suspicion of spying.

88-year-old grandmother Edna Jester was arrested in 2008 for refusing to return a football to a neighbour's son. Mrs Jester had lived in the same house in Blue Ash, Cincinnati since 1949. She was charged with petty theft.

Neil McArdle was jailed for 12 months after making a hoax bomb threat. He had forgotten to book a wedding venue and daren't tell his fiancé, he thought the bomb hoax would cover up the mistake.

Holly Crawford from Pennsylvania was arrested for cruelty after advertising Goth Kittens on the internet. Her kittens were pierced and studded in their ears, necks and tails.

A man was arrested, and later fined, in Portsmouth, UK, for pretending to be a ghost and shouting 'Woooooo' at mourners in a graveyard. Anthony Stalled (24) said he had been drinking prior to the incident.

While being fingerprinted and awaiting a breath test at South Charleston police HQ, West Virginia, 34-year-old Jose Cruz lifted his leg and passed wind loudly in the direction of Patrolman T.E. Parsons. Cruz was charged with assault and is the only person I can find to have been arrested for farting. (See Petomane)

Nicolas Wigg has to be high on the list of the world's dumbest criminals. He was arrested after leaving himself logged on to Facebook on a computer at a house he'd burgled.

ART AND ARTISTS

Manet's famous painting of the bar at the Folies Bergère is the only known famous work of art featuring two bottles of Bass beer.

Matisse's artwork 'Le Bateau' ('The Boat') hung upside down in the New York Museum of Modern Art for almost seven weeks before anyone noticed.

This piece of information is often quoted by critics to suggest Matisse's cut-paper design was some kind of worthless abstract splodge. In fact the picture depicts a boat sailing above its almost identical reflection in the water. It looks just as good whichever way up it is viewed.

Michelangelo is frequently said to have designed the colourful uniforms of the Swiss Guard who patrol outside St Peter's and the Vatican. One source claims the only modification to Michelangelo's original design came in 1975 when a pocket for tear-gas grenades was added.

The uniforms are, in fact, based on armour common throughout Europe during the Renaissance period and there is absolutely no evidence linking Michelangelo with their design.

Monte Carlo Casino's smoking lounge has a classical-looking ceiling decorated with paintings of voluptuous, naked ladies. Close inspection shows them to be smoking cigars. (See Man Who Broke the Bank)

In 1930 the US government banned all mail from Spain bearing stamps depicting Goya's famous painting 'The Naked Maja'.

Sculptor Auguste Rodin was in poverty and applied to the French government for a grant to find suitable accommodation. His request was turned down and, in 1917, he died of frostbite in an unheated garret.

Although the government turned down Rodin's request for aid they kept his valuable sculptures warm in museums.

The young Pablo Picasso kept warm by burning his paintings.

Pablo Picasso ordered his mistresses to wrestle and he would make love to the winner.

In 1912 Georges Braque's painting 'Still-Life with Harp and Violin' became the first work by a living artist to hang in the Louvre.

Despite his modern popularity Paul Cezanne died alone of pneumonia in 1906. He was surrounded by crates of unsold paintings and unpaid bills.

Blur's 'Country House' video was directed by artist Damien Hirst.

Vincent van Gogh had a brother, also called Vincent van Gogh, who died at birth.

Myth has it that camel-hair artists' brushes, which are usually made from squirrel hair and contain no camel hair, took their name from having been invented by a Mr Camel. Research has revealed no such person. Camel-hair brushes can be traced back to ancient China and probably did originally contain hair from camels.

The title of the painting universally known as 'Whistler's Mother' is 'Arrangement in Grey and Black No 1: The Artist's Mother.'

ARTHUR

Many places in Britain attract tourists thanks to their connection with the legendary King Arthur and his Knights of the Round Table. Historical support for the actual existence of Arthur is extremely sparse but the public are still willing to cling on to any link with Arthur no matter how slender.

Arthur's Seat is the summit of a hill in the Holyrood district of Edinburgh. The area is approximately 1.5 km in diameter and was once used for archery practice. In Gaelic the ground was called 'Ard-na-said', meaning the 'height of arrows'. 'Ard-na-said' sounds suspiciously like 'Arthur's Seat' if said in a Scottish accent after a couple of pints of heavy.

Tintagel thrives on its Arthurian tourist industry. Selfies are snapped outside King Arthur's Hall. King Arthur's Hall was built in the 1930s by a custard powder magnate.

At the time of writing in 2017 a new archaeological dig at Tintagel Castle, a ruin on the headland, has discovered remains dating to the fifth century with pottery and glass suggesting a possible royal connection.

The Arthurian link with Tintagel originated in around 1136. Geoffrey of Monmouth's 'Historia Regum Britanniae' sees Gorlois, Duke of Cornwall, install his wife, Ingrain, in 'Tintagol' when he went to war. Wizard Merlin disguised Uther Pendragon as Gorlois and Uther impregnated Ingrain who gave birth to Arthur.

Glastonbury is now best known for the rock festival that isn't held there. Pilton, some seven miles from the famed Somerset town, is the home of the festival.

Glastonbury is a place of many mysteries making it a mecca for the world's remaining hippies and a location where Arthurian legends take centre stage as historical facts.

Following a catastrophic fire in 1184 much of the ancient abbey was destroyed. It took only four years for a partial reconstruction permitting services to take place but building work soon ground to a halt.

By 1191 pilgrims had virtually stopped visiting the abbey, not only depleting necessary funds to keep the resident monks in the life style to which they had become accustomed but also the inns and lodging houses that still stand outside the Abbey grounds were suffering.

Fortuitously it was at this very time the tombs of King Arthur and Queen Guinevere were discovered in the Abbey cemetery and the pilgrims flocked back.

Some say the dig was inspired by information obtained from an ancient Welsh Bard by Henry II. Others say the dig began when a monk died after expressing a wish to be buried on that exact spot. Most say it was an outrageous but very successful publicity stunt.

Thousands still flock to Glastonbury Abbey (at the time of writing adult entrance fee is £7.50), most head straight for the place where the two graves are marked out on the ground. You might even be lucky enough to find a guide who will tell you all about the plaque (now missing), discovered with the male body, declaring this to be King Arthur 'buried in Avalon' and, of course, as in many such stories, Guinevere retained her beautiful, long, blonde hair that crumbled and disappeared as soon as it was exposed to the air.

Anyone who knows their myths will instantly write-off the Abbey tombs' authenticity because it is common knowledge that Arthur and his Knights are not dead, they merely sleep soundly beneath Glastonbury Tor waiting to spring to the aid of the country in its hour of need.

Arthur was reportedly attracted to Glastonbury by the legend that Joseph of Arametha visited there with the young Jesus. After Christ's ministry and death Joseph returned to Glastonbury where he built a small chapel around which the Abbey was constructed. He brought with him the Holy Grail, the cup used at the Last Supper which was used to catch some of Christ's blood as he died on the cross. The Grail is somewhere beneath the Tor having been dropped down the Chalice Well, another tourist attraction. (See Zodiac)

The Scilly Isles to the west of Cornwall are claimed to be the remains of the lost kingdom of Lyonesse. Lyonesse is yet another final resting place of King Arthur.

Dozmary Pool, Bodmin Moor, Cornwall is claimed as the spot where the knight Bedivere followed Arthur's instructions to dispose of his magical sword, Excalibur. A white-clad woman's arm appeared from the apparently bottomless lake, clasped the sword and disappeared back beneath the surface.

King Arthur is said to have elected upon a round table to give everyone equal status. Winchester Castle displays what is claimed to be King Arthur's Round Table. A tabletop hanging on the castle wall names various members of Arthur's court but the king pictured on the table is almost certainly Henry VIII. Dendrochronology (dating by the rings in the wood) shows the tabletop to have originally been constructed between 1250 and 1280 during the reign of Edward I. Edward was known to have been an Arthur enthusiast who had several round tables made for his own use.

Arthurian tournaments were popular for many years and this tabletop was almost certainly made to celebrate such a tournament then repainted by order of Henry VIII for the state visit of Holy Roman Emperor Charles V in 1522.

If you believe any of the above proves a link with a King called Arthur you'll believe anything.

ARTICHOKE ATTACK

Passengers leaving the ferry from Plymouth at Roscoff invariably avoid driving into this delightful Breton town, heading instead direct for sunny Mediterranean beaches hundreds of miles to the south.

Roscoff has one main street, charmingly cobbled and with a plethora of decent restaurants and bars. Thankfully none of them serving the Full English or Bangers and Mash with Heinz Beans. The standard fare here is anything that comes out of the sea. However most of it doesn't come from their sea, it comes from ours.

If drivers leaving that ferry weren't so obsessive about finding the first cheap wine and tobacco emporium along their road to the South they might have noticed that amongst their fellow passengers on the car decks were several massive articulated trucks decorated with fishy logos.

You would be hard pressed to find a Fruit de Mer along the coasts of Devon or Cornwall, sightings of native langoustines in Scotland are rarer than sightings of the Loch Ness Monster, but here in France and on into Spain the local populace devour the harvest from our waters with an appetite suggesting such luxuries might soon be added to the endangered species list, which indeed they might.

So what do we get in return?

Onions and artichokes!

In the cause of research I could not taste any difference between Roscoff onions and British onions but theirs attract a premium price due to being sold by Onion Johnnies. These are the guys on rusty old bikes who gave us our stereotypical image of Frenchmen as unshaven rogues wearing stripy shirts and black berets. The onions are shipped over to the U.K. by the container-load and the Johnnies make a daily collection of as many strings of the things as they can hang from their bikes and around their necks and then pedal off to sell these to British housewives who melt at their Gallic accents and Gauloises/garlic scented breath.

I once met an Onion Johnny in Roscoff who knew the names of every woman in my home village in Devon. He knew all their dogs and cats, the colours of their front doors, when they last had their bedrooms redecorated and at what time their husbands arrived home from work.

Then there are the artichokes.

Artichokes come in two varieties. The Jerusalem Artichoke

is the tuber of a species of sunflower. TV chefs describe it as 'versatile', meaning it has little or no flavour so can be boiled then used to pad out a plate of just about anything.

The Globe Artichoke is a member of the thistle family. The fields of Brittany and Normandy are full of the things. Sacks of Globe Artichokes are stacked along the sides of roads for motorists heading south to add to their stash of cheap booze and tobacco. Something French and cheap. One Euro for half a ton.

After boiling, half a ton of Globe Artichokes take something like three months to prepare for eating. Pull off the leaves, cut out the choke and three large sacks full produce approximately a teaspoon of almost edible matter.

But, and I do know I shouldn't begin a sentence with a conjunction, but this is a big BUT. After eating all our best fish and then ripping us off by charging crazy prices for onions the French send us Globe Artichokes.

These are packaged in twos, displayed in plastic trays, wrapped in clingfilm. The price of that duo of mostly inedible green stuff in a U.K. supermarket works out at about the same as you would pay for an entire city's supply in France.

Fields throughout Britain's West Country where dairy cows and beef cattle once roamed are now full of caravans, tacky theme parks and homes for retired donkeys. The climate in this area is virtually the same as in Brittany so why don't our farmers get back to farming? They could grow onions for all those lycra-clad cyclists causing accidents on British roads to peddle to French housewives while pedalling around France and we could pay off the National Debt by sending them globe artichokes at 50p per sackful.

AUSTRALIA

Conveniently ignoring the fact they have ten sheep for every human, ask any Australian what is their main tourist attraction and they'll tell you not to miss the Sydney Harbour Bridge. This structure is based on the Tyne Bridge in Newcastle Upon Tyne and, despite what any Australian tells you it isn't and never was the longest bridge in the world. (See Bridges)

Australia's greatest artist is regularly said to be Russell Drysdale. Drysdale was from Bognor Regis in England. Australia's other most famous artist, Tom Roberts, was from Dorset.

Australia's sole contributions to international cuisine are the lamington and alcopops. A lamington is a sponge cake covered in a thin layer of chocolate then dipped in desiccated coconut, alcopops resulted from someone having more lemons than he could sell.

Australia does have some unique animals. I am reliably informed that most of them smell and are flea-ridden. Ask anyone from outside the country to name Australia's most famous animal and they're likely to say the kangaroo.

Aborigines hunting in the Outback were approached by explorer Captain Cook who asked them for the name of the strange-looking creatures they were following.

Obviously the Aborigines had no knowledge of English and in their own language they told him: 'We don't understand you.'

'We don't understand you,' in native Aborigine is 'Kangaroo.'

A duck-billed platypus has no stomach and no nipples. It feeds its young with milk that flows from its body.

Australia's first police force included their best-behaved convicts.

Australia produced the world's first test-tube twins in 1981. They also produced the first test-tube triplets and quads. (See Twins)

Red Kangaroos produce two different types of milk from adjacent teats enabling them to feed younger and older offspring at the same time.

Australia's East Alligator River is misnamed. It contains crocodiles not alligators.

Emus cannot walk backwards.

AUTOGRAPHS

Rudyard Kipling was reputed to earn £5 for every word he wrote. After several attempts to acquire the great writer's autograph an enthusiast sent Kipling £5. He received a one-word reply, 'Thanks'.

Albert Einstein was always reluctant to give autographs so he charged a dollar to sign anything and donated the funds to charity.

AWARD CEREMONIES

For 25 years I wrote the questions for the many U.K. editions of Trivial Pursuit and, as a result, I was a regular on TV and radio chat shows. I suppose hearing someone selling board games made a change from people selling books.

I gained something of a reputation for my ability to reply to boring questions with amusing ripostes, leading to guest spots on 'celebrity' quiz shows, a weekly slot on a morning pop programme and countless invitations to take part in charity events.

To contribute properly to charities I've always thought it necessary to limit one's resources to as few organisations as possible. I gave most of my time to a local charity for mentally handicapped children but was intrigued when invited to become a director of the Dead Comics Society.

This organisation was based in London and its initial aim was to erect blue plaques on the homes of deceased British comedy stars. Celebrities who had been involved in the career of the person to be celebrated were invited along to witness the unveiling of the plaque with the best known of them making a speech and pulling the string. This was followed by a lunch, raffle and auction with the resulting profits going to a charity selected either by the string puller or a member of the dead comic's family.

My only fellow director with any sense of humour was Jack Douglas, famed for his twitch and appearances in 'Carry On' movies. It wasn't long before this humourless bunch had a major fallout and split into two separate organisations. I went along with the Jack Douglas faction now re-named the British Comedy Society.

The British Comedy Society is a great name. It sounds very official and we never had any problem attracting string pullers. We then branched out from dead comics to living ones, handing out British Comedy Society Living Legend Awards to the likes of Ken Dodd, June Whitfield and Peter Sallis.

Of course from 1990 to 2014 the British Comedy Awards were an annual feature on TV. The British Comedy Society had absolutely nothing to do with this prestigious award but, thanks to our name, I never had any problem obtaining invitations.

Someone once described the Academy Awards TV coverage as 'Five minutes of entertainment crammed into a four-hour show.' I'm informed by someone who watched the British Comedy Awards on TV that it had a similarly soporific affect to that of watching cricket.

Before the ceremony started the entire audience was force fed drinks. Girls handed out packets of cigarettes and cigars in a room decorated with No Smoking signs. It always raised a laugh when you were told you could not take your drink into the theatre. The glass was taken out of your hand as you arrived at the door then replaced with a full one at the other side.

A room full of inebriated celebrities was always a recipe for chaos and the Comedy Awards are probably best remembered for the occasions when Caroline Aherne heckled Sir Nigel Hawthorne, Kevin Bishop threw a bottle at the Inbetweeners and Julian Clary made a sexually explicit joke about a Tory politician.

I cannot remember a single person who received an award during the many years I attended but I can remember some of the presenters. Politicians, Hollywood royalty and sports stars made surprise appearances to open a golden envelope and read out the winner of a particular category.

I was once involved in a backstage fracas when boxer Evander Holyfield, fresh from his ear-biting fight with Mike Tyson, rescued Jonathan Ross from Placido Domingo who had failed to see any humour in Ross' introduction of him when he walked on to hand over a trophy.

Loretta Swit (Hotlips Houlihan from 'M*A*S*H') scoffed mini fish and chips from a paper cone while I held her glass of champagne, I danced and sang reggae with Secretary of State for Northern Ireland Mo Mowlam, and the truly legendary Jane Russell let me into a secret that involved a re-write of a Trivial Pursuit question. (See BRAS)

I was at the British Comedy Awards when Spike Milligan famously referred to Prince Charles as a 'grovelling bastard' and should have realised from this that Spike was not going to be easy to handle when we invited him to unveil a plaque in honour of Peter Sellers at Elstree Studios.

Everyone knew we wanted Spike, every comedian's favourite comedian, to unveil this tribute to his most famous co-star but he had failed to attend several other events due to illness and we doubted he would come to our luncheon.

One day I arrived home from my regular afternoon visit to the pub to be greeted by my son with the news that Spike Milligan had just phoned. My first thought was that this was probably a wind-up, everyone can do a Milligan Goon impression, even Prince Charles. However, I checked the phone number and it was from the area in Sussex where I knew Spike lived, so, with a shaking hand, I made the call.

Spike said he would be happy to unveil the plaque, we arranged for one of our directors with a posh car to collect him at nine in the morning to get to us for the noon ceremony.

Then the daily calls began. Despite the adulation he received from everyone in his profession I think Spike was a lonely man. He checked the date and time for his collection every day, he confirmed that his wife, Paddy, was invited. He talked about things he'd watched on television and he regularly chatted about cricket. I am not a fan of cricket but I took to checking the scores each morning so I could join in with my hero's love for the game.

On the day of the event I had a call from my fellow-director to say he was outside Spike's house and Spike said I'd told him they weren't setting off until ten so he was still in his pyjamas. They arrived at the studio an hour late, Spike pulled the string to unveil the plaque and mumbled a few words about Peter Sellers that only I heard.

We seated him at the front of the star-studded studio restaurant and he quickly let us know he would not be eating but would like a pot of tea. I asked him how long he would be speaking when he got on to the stage and he made it very clear he would not be getting on the stage and he would not be saying a word.

Burt Kwouk who played Cato opposite Peter Sellers' Inspector Clouseau character agreed to say a few words and Shirley Eaton, who appeared on screen with Sellers also agreed to share her memories.

I had read a few very funny stories about the antics Spike and Sellers had got up to so it was left to me to hold the show together. Never in my wildest dreams did I ever think I would be standing on a stage raising laughs in front of Spike Milligan. I had already realised that Spike was not the kind of person to do anything for the sake of correctness or image and I was over the moon to see him laughing uproariously at my telling of his stories.

This was one of Spike Milligan's final public appearances. (See EPITAPHS)

Until 1989 Oscar winners were announced with the words: 'And the winner is …', this was then changed to 'And the Oscar goes to …' to avoid offending losers.

In 1929 the first Oscar was a Best Actor Award for Emil Jannings. He didn't bother turning up to collect it.

The British porn industry has annual awards called the SHAFTAS.

A driver in Ealing crashed his van on his way home from a ceremony where he had been awarded a prize for safe driving.

Although Oscar statuettes have been sold at auction winners agree that if they don't want to keep their Oscar they will sell it back to the Academy for a token one dollar.

Oscar Hammerstein II, music-writing partner of Richard Rodgers, is the only Oscar to have won an Oscar.

BANKS AND BANKERS

'A banker is a fellow who lends you his umbrella when the sun is shining and wants it back when it begins to rain'. — Mark Twain

A customer wrote his own terms for accepting a credit card then successfully sued his bank when they broke his terms.

The town of Tightwad in Missouri is served by the Tightwad Bank.

When the author of this book was charged £50 by a bank for a letter from the Manager I replied to the letter and, as a professional writer, sent them a £60 invoice for my letter and warned I would reply to all future mail and charge accordingly. They paid up without question and sent me no more bills for their letters.

Charles (Pretty Boy) Floyd found fame as a bank robber during America's Great Depression. Pretty Boy was loved by the public because when he robbed a bank he always made a point of destroying any mortgage contracts he could find.

In 1995 two men robbed a bank in Pittsburgh and were soon arrested thanks to CCTV. They were shocked to discover they had been spotted by the cameras, explaining that, as children, they'd made invisible ink from lemon juice so prior to the robbery they had rubbed this on their faces thinking it would make them invisible to the cameras.

Ren Xiaofeng, a branch manager at The Agricultural Bank of China, stole $26,000 from the bank with the intention of buying lottery tickets and using his hoped-for winnings to pay off his theft. Against all odds he won, so he tried again with $6.7 million. He lost all but $95,000 and was sentenced to death.

In the year 2000, the Zimbabwe Banking Corporation lottery was won by Robert Mugabe, the President of Zimbabwe. (See Tale of Two Accents)

Some banks in Italy will accept Parmigiana Reggiano cheese as collateral against loans. Temperature controlled bank vaults hold hundreds of thousands of the cheeses which take at least two years to mature. (See Cheese)

Stock brokers famously use hand signals to communicate and most of these remain a mystery to anyone outside their clique. The hand signal for the Deutsche Bank is the index finger held horizontally beneath the nose, a reference to Hitler's moustache. (See Hitler)

'Compound interest is the most powerful force on Earth.' — Albert Einstein

The people most frequently shot dead in US bank robberies are bank robbers.

BARRIERS

Approximately 100 years prior to the birth of Donald Trump, Tsar Nicholas II wanted to build an electric fence around Russia.

The Berlin Wall (1961 to 1989) was 28 miles long and had a height varying between 11 and 13 feet.

In 1989 Margaret Thatcher asked Soviet President Mikhail Gorbachev not to let the Berlin Wall fall. She was afraid a unified Germany would disrupt the balance of power in Europe.

Labourers working on the Great Wall of China were fed mostly on a type of sauerkraut.

The Great Wall of China was mostly funded by a state lottery.

Offa's Dyke, an earthwork roughly along the border between England from Wales, was constructed 200 years before King Offa was born. (See Tale of Two Accents)

The Western or Wailing Wall is the most-visited site in Jerusalem. It is venerated as the only remaining part of the ancient Holy Temple. (See Mail)

Hadrian's Wall at 73 miles is the longest wall in Europe. It was built by the Romans to keep Scottish tribes from attacking their colony, Britannia.

BATHROOMS

I know my son will thank me for this memory! The first time I ever had to buy a bathroom suite we checked out Homebase and my son went missing. We eventually found him sitting on a toilet in the middle of the store with his trousers round his ankles.

When I was a child we didn't have a bathroom. The lavatory was in a stone outhouse at the bottom of the garden. The Radio Times magazine was torn into half pages that were impaled on a large, rusty nail at the back of the door, a candle provided the only light for nighttime visits and for three months of the year the whole system was frozen solid. Instead of water you got a 'clunk' when you pulled the chain.

Baths were taken weekly in a zinc tub in front of the kitchen fire. The bath took hours to fill with hot water being added a kettle and a pan at a time. The family took it in turns. Kids first and then to bed before mum and dad took their turn.

Americans call a public W.C. a bathroom and there's always a ten-inch gap under the door. A British bathroom contains a bath, a lavatory and a washbasin, cross the Channel and you can add a bidet.

Since the sixties we Brits have added a shower over the bath, in the eighties many baths were replaced with showers and now we have discovered wet rooms.

My big complaint is that nobody has ever come up with a standard size for bathroom furniture.

As a senior citizen I have never understood why some lavatory seats are at a sensible height from the ground so you only need to lower yourself a couple of inches and then raise yourself this same distance after completing your business but other toilet seats are so close to the ground that a block and tackle is required to get down and back up again. (See Poo)

Baths were once avocado, mushroom or peach, most people in the 21st century go for white but, whatever the colour, has anyone ever wondered who designed the bathtub?

When avocado, mushroom and peach were in favour it was also fashionable for baths to be boxed in. I remember my dad constructing a cage from 2 inch by two inch pine and then covering this with hardboard that was given a coat of maroon paint, left over from the front door. This was at the same time beautifully panelled doors were all given a hardboard coat and estate agents' descriptions listed 'boxed-in baths and flush doors' as a plus factor.

Now the hardboard has been ripped away from most doors and baths, the original structure is a selling point. I understand the attraction of panelled doors but what is it that attracts people to those dreadful cast iron legs on bathtubs?

Why are bath's elevated from the floor? As you get older and your legs become less functional you will realise that getting into a bath is no problem at all but when you are wet and slippery lowering your first, aged leg that extra few inches to the ground is a procedure that takes on the proportions of climbing from a barstool down to a pub floor awash with ale after one more than you promised yourself you were going to consume.

Once the first wet leg has reached the ground the second leg has to come out. Maybe this is why the woman on the TV bath commercial wears a swimsuit so she's decently covered when she lands on the floor and calls for help. (See Afternoon TV)

Frank Sinatra was a cleanliness fanatic and is known to have taken as many as twelve showers in a day.

BATTY

After World War II it was reported that more than 20 million bats had been collected by the US Army Air Corps in 1943 as part of a scheme to develop a bat bomb.

The idea was to release bats into enemy territory where they would take up residence in enemy lofts before a timing device exploded an incendiary bomb strapped to the bats' backs.

After a $2 million investment in the project, the idea was dropped following practice runs during which bats carrying live bombs took up residence in an American aircraft hangar and in the general's car.

Bats pollinate agave plants from which tequila is made.

The logo on a bottle of Bacardi rum is a fruit bat.

Male Dayak fruit bats lactate.

There are over 1,000 species of bats. Three species of vampire bat feed solely on blood.

Bats account for 23% of known animals by species.

Bat species include the wrinkle-faced bat, the Antillean ghost-faced bat and the thumbless bat.

A 2009 bat survey revealed that bats are as likely to turn right as left when leaving their cave, despite it being an 'established fact' for many years that they always turn to the left.

Male bats have a higher rate of homosexuality than any other animal.

BEASTLY PUNISHMENTS

Mary, a five-ton elephant, is the last known animal to be hanged for murder. On September 13th (unlucky for Mary) 1916, Spark Circus paraded through the small town of Kingsport, Tennessee. Walter Eldridge, a temporary trainer, prodded Mary's head with a pointed stick when she reached out to pick up a piece of fruit from the side of the road.

Mary lifted the man with her trunk from where he was sitting on her back, smashed him against a soft-drinks kiosk and then stood on his head.

A member of the crowd pumped five bullets into Mary but she survived to appear in that evening's show.

The following day in the town of Erwin, the Circus' next stop, the authorities decided that Mary should hang. She was taken to a nearby railway yard where a large crowd watched as a chain was placed around her neck and she was hoisted into the air by a crane.

The first chain snapped and was replaced by one of a heavier gauge, this resulted in what was described as 'a quick death'.

A pig was publicly executed in 1386 for killing a child.

In 1740 a French cow was hanged after being found guilty of witchcraft.

Two dogs were hanged for witchcraft during the Salem witch trials.

BEATLES

When John Lennon was shown a list of 169 songs credited to the partnership of Lennon/McCartney he said 75 of these were his own solo efforts. He told a reporter from music magazine 'Record Mirror' that 70 of the songs had been written by Paul McCartney and only 27 had any element of collaboration. (Yes I know that's a total of 172, not 169, but it's John Lennon's arithmetic not mine.)

'A Hard Day's Night' is the only Beatles album to exclusively contain compositions by Lennon and McCartney.

Lennon and McCartney provide backing vocals on the Rolling Stones' 'We Love You.'

Paul McCartney's first name is James.

The best selling Beatles album in the USA is 'Abbey Road.'

The last time all four Beatles recorded together was on August 20th 1969 when they completed 'I Want You (She's So Heavy)'.

It has been claimed the semaphore letters signalled by the Beatles on the sleeve of the 'Help!' album spell out H-E-L-P. In fact they are the apparently random N-U-J-V.

The stereo recording of 'Lucy In the Sky With Diamonds' is a semitone higher than the mono version, hence it is slightly faster.

'I Am the Walrus' was banned by the BBC because it mentions 'knickers'.

'You have to be a bastard to make it, and that's a fact. And the Beatles are the biggest bastards on earth.' — John Lennon

BEN HUR

'Ben Hur' won eleven Oscars. It was banned in China as pro-Christian propaganda and in Italy because the Roman doesn't win the chariot race.

Despite many claims from those who possibly have much better eyesight than myself, I have carefully studied the 'Ben Hur' chariot race and there is no sign of a red car driving down a hillside in the background.

Judah and Mescal ride horses on saddles with stirrups in one of the early scenes in the movie. In actuality it would be another 700 years before stirrups were introduced in Europe.

Someone says 'Wow' in the film. This word was first used in Scotland in the 16th century.

Traders empty baskets of chili peppers as Judas walks through the market. Chili peppers were introduced to Europe by a physician on Columbus' second voyage in 1493.

Welsh actor Hugh Griffith won the Best Supporting Actor Oscar for his role as Sheik Ilderim. In the movie Griffith refers to 'the beard of the Prophet.' The prophet in question is Mohammad who was born 600 years after the period in which 'Ben Hur' is set.

BEVERAGES

In 1930 the US Supreme Court ruled that the brand name 'Coke' belongs to Coca-Cola.

In some US states Highway Patrol cars carry a two-gallon container of Coke as this is effective for washing blood from roadways after accidents.

When Coca-Cola was launched in China the company used Chinese characters that sounded like 'Coca-Cola'. Unfortunately the literal meaning of the symbols was 'Bite the wax tadpole.' Early sales of the drink were understandably somewhat sluggish.

After Coke and Pepsi the world's best-selling soft drink brand is Orange Fanta.

Coffee was originally advertised in 17th century London as a cure for gout and scurvy.

Mascaraocofea Vianneyi, Madagascan coffee, is naturally without caffeine. Most so-called caffeine-free coffees and teas contain a small amount of caffeine.

Caffeine extracted from coffee and tea to make so-called decaffeinated drinks is sold to soft drinks companies.

Iceland's signature drink, Brennivin, is made from potatoes.

The drinking straw celebrated its one hundredth birthday in 1988.

Doctor Pepper was originally sold as 'liquid sunshine.'

Japan has a popular soft drink called Mucos.

Pee Cola is popular in Ghana.

Experts say perfect coffee requires 17.42 units of water to each unit of coffee.

Dandelion roots were roasted and used as a coffee substitute during World War II.

The only water Queen Elizabeth II ever drinks is bottled Malvern Water which is transported with her to wherever she goes in the world.

BIBLICAL

The Bible is the world's most shoplifted book.

In the Bible, Eve eats 'the fruit of the tree'. There is no mention of an apple.

The Bible makes no mention of Three Wise Men or Three

Kings. The assumption that Baby Jesus was visited by a royal or educated trio stems from the three gifts, gold, frankincense and myrrh. These gifts might have been delivered by two visitors or even by a much larger group.

Ehud's only claim to fame is that he's first left-handed person in the Bible.

Cheese is mentioned three times in the Bible. (See Cheese)

The only nuts mentioned in the Bible are almonds and pistachios.

Pepper isn't mentioned at all in the Bible but salt crops up 41 times.

There is no reference to angels singing anywhere in the Bible.

There are seven suicides in the Bible. Ten people are raised from the dead.

Methuselah is the oldest man in the Bible at 969 years.

The golden calf Aaron makes for the Israelites was made entirely from recycled earrings.

The Bible warns there will be no marriages in Heaven.

There are 41 references to dogs in the Bible but not a single mention of a cat.

In the Book of Kings a man called Ben-hur was a deputy over Israel. (See Ben Hur)

Sarah is the only woman who laughs in the Bible.

Ivory is mentioned thirteen times in the Bible but there is no mention of elephants.

Job reports that his wife thought he had bad breath.

Despite all the classical paintings and references in other books, nowhere in the Bible does it say Delilah cut Samson's hair. She let somebody else do it for her.

Four women stood by the cross as Jesus was dying and three of them were called Mary.

The word 'Christian' is only used twice in the Bible, the plural, 'Christians', appears once..

The Book of Esther makes no mention of God.

The first colour mentioned in the Bible is green.

Noah's Ark had only one window.

After the destruction of the Temple of Baal the Israelites used it as a latrine.

A 1999 survey revealed that 9% of Americans believed Joan of Arc was Noah's wife.

For other Biblical facts see Religion

BINGO

The most popular pen colour used by bingo players is purple. A bingo pen is known as a dauber.

New York toy salesman Edwin S. Lowe invented the bingo card. He worked with mathematician Carl Leffler to devise more than 6,000 number combinations.

UK bingo cards have three rows of nine columns. US bingo cards are five squares by five squares.

UK bingo numbers go from 1 to 90. US bingo numbers go from 1 to 75.

In the early 19th century bingo cards were used as a mathematics aid in German schools.

80% of people who go out to play bingo are women. 83% of online bingo players are women.

The first online bingo game was 'Bingo Zone' launched in 1996.

One in five Scots play bingo but only one in twenty in the South East of England.

More money is spent on bingo in the UK each year than is spent watching football.

The average 90-ball bingo game lasts four minutes.

Bingo was an old slang word for brandy.

Bingo was originally called Beano because beans were used to cover the numbers. It is claimed the name change came when a woman excitedly shouted 'Bingo' after winning a jackpot.

The Queen and Prince Philip enjoy playing bingo at family parties.

Bing Crosby's childhood nickname was Bingo.

BIRDS OF A FEATHER

There are over 9,500 species of birds and two-thirds of these species are found only in tropical rain forests.

There are more plastic flamingos in the USA than real ones.

Flamingoes pair for life. Some have been known to stay with their mates for more than 40 years in zoos, 20 years in the wild .

There has never been such a thing as a robin with a red breast. A robin's breast feathers are orange.

America's national bird, the Bald Eagle, is not bald. It takes its name because it is piebald, or black and white.

When ducks sleep in groups the ones on the outside keep an eye open to watch for potential trouble.

The whistling swan has the most feathers with 25,000. The tiny hummingbird can have as few as 1,000.

In cities birds start the dawn chorus up to five hours earlier than in the countryside.

The world's commonest bird is the red-billed Quelea. Mostly living in sub-Saharan Africa. there are an estimated 1.5 billion breeding pairs.

The seagulls in Alfred Hitchcock's movie, 'The Birds,' were fed wheat soaked in whiskey to keep them standing around and not flying too much.

To keep them light enough to fly most birds do not have a bladder. The droppings produced by birds are a combination of faeces and urine. (See Poo) (See Urine)

The Kiwi has feathers that feel like hair, nostrils on the tip of their beak, which they use to sniff for insects in the ground then snort to clear, and heavy bones filled with marrow. Add to this their inability to fly and it's clear why they are often referred to as 'honorary animals.'

The kiwi lays the biggest egg compared with the size of the bird. Weighing in at approximately a pound it is one-third the size of the mother bird.

Approximately the same size as billiard balls, ostriches have the biggest eyes of any land creature.

Alligators have been known to balance a stick on the end of their nose to attract tasty birds seeking nesting material.

BLOOMING CRAZY

In 1983 Britain in Bloom judges said a combination of heat and a very long, hard day could have been to blame for their slight error of judgement.

They had just awarded the certificate for Second Prize to a slot machine arcade at Dawlish Warren, in Devon, only to be told by Tony Riches, the arcade's jubilant owner, that every item in his magnificent floral display was made from plastic.

Brixham Horticultural Show's major awards were almost all won by Mrs A.M.C. Mallowan in 1959. Mrs Mallowan did admit that her 18 first prizes, six seconds, three thirds, a bronze medal and four cups were won with the help of a head gardener and his three assistants but this didn't prevent a reporter from the local press suggesting that the lady's success would encourage members of the public to read any book she might produce on the subject of gardening.

The reporter's published account includes the line: 'Mrs Mallowan obviously has her hands full with her hobby of gardening without having to squeeze in time to write.'

Mrs A.M.C. Mallowan is better known by the name Agatha Christie.

Dedicated gardeners will tell you to water plants in the early morning or after sunset but few of them can tell you why. Drops of water act like tiny magnifying glasses and can concentrate the sun's rays on to leaves and blossoms causing unsightly burn marks.

BOGEY

Humphrey Bogart is listed at number-one on the American Film Institute's list of the greatest screen actors.

'Never Say Goodbye', a 1946 film, had women swooning in the aisles when it ended with heart throb Errol Flynn singing a few bars of 'Remember Me.' The singing voice was that of an uncredited Humphrey Bogart who was also the anonymous voice of Flynn when he was required to adopt the image off a tough guy.

With an eye to image, Warner Brothers publicity always claimed Humphrey Bogart was born on Christmas Day. He was born on 23rd January 1899.

Bogey had a lisp.

BOTTOMS

Many breeds of turtle can breathe through their bottoms. (See Petomane)

In 1920 baseball player Clarence Blethen retired injured from a game after biting himself on the bottom with the false teeth he kept in his back pocket.

For his final three months President James Garfield had to be fed through his anus.

In 2012 the New Zealand government took legal action to prevent a couple from calling their child Anal.

A 25-million-year-old fossilised cockroach was discovered with a parasitic worm sticking out of its bottom.

BRAS

In 2009 a respected medical journal warned that bras can cause injuries to young men. The first recorded serious case of injury by bra came when a young man was admitted to a London hospital and had to undergo surgery to repair a fracture and ligament damage suffered in an attempt to remove his girlfriend's bra.

The journal went on to quote statistics from a poll it financed revealing that 40% of men between the ages of 18 and 25 have such a poor knowledge of how to unfasten a bra that they are at risk of suffering injuries.

The bra strap clip was invented and patented by author Mark Twain.

The cone bra designed by Jean-Paul Gaultier for Madonna's 'Blonde Ambition' tour sold at Christie's in London for £48,000.

The Landmark Theatre in Ifracombe, Devon, has two cone-shaped roofs and is know to all as Madonna's Bra.

Early Canadian editions of Trivial Pursuit claimed the bra was invented by Otto Titzling. Funny but not correct. The term 'brassiere' was first used by a New York newspaper in 1893 and the first patent for a modern bra was secured by American model Mary Phelps Jacob in 1914 but we have to go back to ancient Greece for evidence of the first cloth breast supports.

When I had a one-to-one with Jane Russel (See Award Ceremonies) she opened the conversation by correctly guessing that I thought she was dead. I would loved to have talked to her about Marilyn Monroe but you can hardly ask one of the two greatest sex icons of the 1950s about the other. As the U.K. Trivial Pursuit question writer I remembered a trivial 'fact' that has appeared in every pub quiz and quiz book since Trivial Pursuit made quizzing popular in the early 1980s.

I asked her if it was true that inventor, pilot, film director and philanthropist Howard Hughes really did design the bra she wore in 'The Outlaw'.

She looked around to make sure we were not being overheard then, in a conspiratorial whisper, she told me that the answer to this was 'Yes and no.'

'Yes' Howard Hughes did design a bra for her to wear in the classic movie. 'It had cantilevered breast lifters made from wires. The wires stuck into me and it was so painful I dumped it in a bin and in the movie I wear my own bra bought from a department store.'

George Lucas told Carrie Fisher that in space her flesh would expand but her bra wouldn't. She would, therefore, be strangled by her bra. She believed him and didn't wear a bra throughout the filming of the first 'Star Wars' movie.

The Emergency Bra, or eBra, is available online and from many stores. The two cups of the bra separate to become gas masks.

The Playtex company made the spacesuits worn by Armstrong and Aldrin when they became the first two men on the moon. (See Men on Moon)

In 1999 there were two recorded cases in Britain of women killed when lightning struck their under-wired bras.

Mainstreet USA in the original DisneyLand included a lingerie store called 'The Wizard of Bras'.

BRIDGES

Famous bridges around the world are based on bridges in Britain. Budapest, capital of Hungary, is now a popular tourist destination with thousands of visitors having photographs taken on the bridge linking Buda to Pest.

Marlow in Buckinghamshire is linked to a nearby village by

a suspension bridge across the Thames. This bridge was built in 1831 and is the prototype for the bridge between Buda and Pest. (See Australia)

Waterloo Bridge across the Thames in London is known as the 'Ladies Bridge' because it was built mostly by women.

(See France)

CAPITALS

The capital of Portugal was Rio de Janeiro for fourteen years during the Napoleonic Wars.

Citizens of and visitors to Berlin consume 125 tons of sausages every day.

By area Tokyo is the world's largest capital city (6,993 square miles).

By population Beijing is the world's largest capital.

In 2016, £100 would buy you a plot of land in London SW3 the size of a credit card.

The full name of Bangkok is Krung Thep Mahanakhon Amon Rattanakosin Mahinthara Ayuthaya Mahadilok Phop Noppharat Ratchathani Burirom Udomratchaniwet Mahasathan Amon Piman Awatan Sathit Sakkathattiya Witsanukam Prasit.

Drivers in Paris are so used to the 'give way to the right' rule that the city only has one STOP sign.

CARLING

Carling lager originated in Canada and has been available in British pubs since 1952. Having been an ale drinker since my teens I have never understood why people would want to drink virtually flavourless fizz. Having been born and brought up in Yorkshire I have never understood why anyone would want to drink something named Carling.

In Yorkshire and much of the North of England the fifth Sunday in Lent was traditionally known as Carling Sunday. This had nothing at all to do with drinking vast quantities of lager.

Carlings (or Carlins in Lancashire) are dried grey or black peas. On the appointed day these were fried in butter and often served with a good sprinkling of malt vinegar. Everyone helped themselves to the dish leaving a few behind to go cold. At the end of the meal unmarried guests took it in turns to pick a pea and the one who took the last one would be the first to marry.

CARS

It takes almost four times more fuel to keep a car's engine idling for one minute than it takes if you turn it off and restart when you're ready to go.

Front seat safety belts were first offered as standard equipment in 1963. Rear seat belts came two years later.

The first 'Guide Michelin' was published in 1900 and consisted mostly of a list of filling stations in France.

In Russia it's a criminal offence to drive a dirty car.

When first introduced cars were seen as a green alternative to the mounds of horse poo being dumped in the streets.

There are 30,000 parts in the average petrol or diesel car. An electric car can have as few as 7,000.

The Honda CR-V was originally supplied with a fold-up picnic table in the boot.

Pregreening is the term for creeping forwards while waiting for a red traffic light to change.

Rolls-Royce claim that 65% of all the cars the company has ever produced are still on the road.

Ralph Teeter who invented cruise control was blind following an accident as a five-year-old.

CELEBRITY SCENE

Jerry Springer was born in Highgate underground station, London and he was once the mayor of Cincinnati.

Johnny Depp, who played Willie Wonka in the 2005 remake of 'Charlie and the Chocolate Factory,' was allergic to chocolate as a child.

Scarlett Johansson has a twin brother called Hunter.

Actor Colin Farrell auditioned to join Boyzone.

Rowan Atkinson, best known as Mr Bean, has a degree in Electrical Engineering.

One Direction singer Liam Payne has a fear of spoons.

Orlando Bloom has a fear of pigs.

Woody Harrelson's father was a hitman who worked for several organised crime syndicates and was convicted of a number of murders.

Bob Marley's father was white. When Bob was born his father was 60 and his mother 18.

Teenaged Christopher Walken ran away to a circus where he trained as a lion tamer.

Michael J. Fox's middle name is Andrew. There was already a Michael A. Fox in the Screen Actor's Guild so he had to change it.

Halle Berry was named after a local department store. Her parents originally called her Maria Halle Berry, Halle's being a department store in their hometown of Cleveland. When she was five-years-old they legally switched the order of her names to make her Halle Maria Berry.

CENSORSHIP

The Chinese word for censorship is banned in China because officially there is no censorship in China.

Until 1978 the works of Shakespeare, Aristotle and Dickens were banned in China.

The town of Empire in California banned the children's book 'Little Red Riding Hood' because a bottle of wine was pictured in the basket of goodies being taken to Grandma and it was said this would encourage kids to drink.

Changes to make it more acceptable to children were made to early editions of 'Little Red Riding Hood' in which the Wolf asks the heroine to remove her clothing one item at a time then join him in bed. She escapes though the bathroom.

Shel Silverstein's book of verse, 'A Light in the Attic' was banned in various parts of the USA. The poem 'How Not to Have to Dry the Dishes,' was said to stimulate disobedience and messiness and an illustration of a child breaking crockery was an obvious encouragement to smash things. More criticism came over a poem describing the death of a girl when her parents refuse to buy her a pony.

'Bambi' was banned by the Nazis because it is by a Jewish author.

Thomas Bowdler rewrote the works of Shakespeare with the rude bits removed. Not only the rude bits, in 'Hamlet' he changes Ophelia's drowning from suicide to an accident.

Belgium is the only country never to have censored adult movies.

The first film to be censored in the UK was a 90-second short showing a slice of Stilton cheese through a microscope. Cheesemakers kicked up a storm at images of bacteria moving within the cheese and the movie was removed from cinemas.

From the sixteenth century to 1966 the Catholic Church maintained a list of forbidden books. More than 4,000 titles made it on to the list.

The BBC banned even the title of Max Romeo's international reggae hit, 'Wet Dream'. Romeo maintained the song was inspired by rain falling on the tin roof of his home in Jamaica.

CHARITABLE

The textile industry in Africa has virtually collapsed due to charitable donations of clothing.

In 2013 the majority of charitable donations in the US (31%) went to religion. Medical research is the most popular cause in the UK receiving 48% of donations.

Australia is the world's most charitable country with two-thirds of the population making a donation or helping a stranger in a typical month. Ireland comes second, Canada third, the UK is at eighth place and the USA comes bottom of the top twenty. (See Australia)

52% of adult charity runners are men, 48% women, but women are more likely to make a donation to charity than men.

The most commonly quoted figure for the number of charities in the UK is 160,000. There are actually more than 400,000. The Charity Commission lists 180,000 charities in England and Wales. In addition to this there are the charities in Scotland and Northern Ireland plus many thousands of charities too small to be registered.

CHEESE

The earliest archaeological evidence for cheese shows it as being made more than 6,000 years ago.

Britain's oldest named cheese is Cheshire, first recorded in 1580.

The most regularly consumed cheese around the world is mozzarella, thanks to its use as a pizza topping.

Although cow's milk is now used for a lot of mozzarella, it is traditionally made from buffalo milk. Mozzarella is a stretched curd cheese.

In 2013, nine babies in the UK were given the first name Cheese.

Cheese is the most regularly shoplifted product in British supermarkets.

Many sources claim the term 'Ploughman's Lunch' was devised in the 1960s by the Milk Marketing Board to boost sales of cheese. The ploughman's is known to date back to the 50s under that name and farmers back as far as the 1890s took bread, cheese and beer, or cider, into the fields for lunch. It is likely the Milk Marketing Board launched their campaign to boost pub lunches after a decline in cheese eating during World War II when cheese was rationed to two ounces per person per week and the only variety available was 'National Cheese' which was like a hard Cheddar.

'Petit Suisse,' (Little Swiss cheese) is not made in Switzerland but in Normandy, France.

American Cheese isn't American and it isn't cheese. The bland, pre-sliced product was developed in the 1950s by the Kraft company in Switzerland who recognised a market for people who put convenience before flavour.

The people of Greece are the world's leading consumers of cheese with an average annual per capita consumption of 27.3 kg, mostly feta.

European law gives Stilton cheese Protected Designation of Origin making it illegal to call anything Stilton if it hasn't been made in the English counties of Derbyshire, Leicestershire or Nottinghamshire. No such law applies to Cheddar which is produced with various degrees of success by factories around the world.

Cassia Marzu is illegal in countries other than Sardinia. This delicacy is putrified cheese purposely infested with live maggots.

Flor de Guia cheese if produced on the island of Grand Canaria in the Canary Islands and can only be made by women.

Brits are the most lactose-tolerant people in the world. (See Feet)

CHILD BRIDES

Every year thousands of children under the age of 18 are married in the USA. Although many states do stick to the minimum age of 18, 27 states do not specify an age below which a child cannot marry.

Between 2000 and 2010 (2010 is the most recent date for which many states can provide data) more than 167,000 children, most of them girls, some as young as twelve, were married in America, most of them to men aged 18 or over.

With twelve states and the District of Columbia unable to provide information on the ages of people married there it is estimated in the above-mentioned decade nearly 248,000 children were married in the USA.

In Idaho a man charged with having sex with a child under the age of 16 can be charged with a felony and imprisoned for up to 25 years. From the states able to produce statistics, Idaho had the highest rate of child marriage between 2000 and 2010 with 55 girls under the age of 16 being married to men 18 or over.

CHINA

'There's no economy in going to bed early to save candles if the result is twins.' — Chinese proverb

China's Great Wall, despite what anyone else might tell you, is not visible with the naked eye from the Moon. Astronauts have said the first evidence of human activity visible from space is the wash from ocean-going ships. (See Barriers)

Mr Kuo, a chef at the Chinese Embassy in London, defected in 1963 and opened the first restaurant in Britain to serve Pekingese dishes including Peking Duck. Prior to this all Chinese restaurants in Britain were Cantonese.

One of the most popular dishes in western Chinese restaurants is Chop Suey. The stir-fried mix of meat and vegetables was invented in California.

A new skyscraper is completed in China every five days.

Hedgehogs are sacred in China.

The Chinese know the Man in the Moon as the Toad in the Moon.

Conservation workers in a Chinese zoo introduced an exercise plan for Pandas because they were putting on too much weight.

China is the world's largest consumer of red wine but it is often served topped up with a soft drink to disguise the flavour.

In 2008 it was reported that melanine, added to milk in China, was causing kidney stones in thousands of children. British MP Peter Mandelson demonstrated his faith in Chinese dairy products by drinking a pint of Chinese liquid yoghurt. The following week he was taken to hospital suffering from kidney stones.

Visitors to China are often disgusted to see men spitting and blowing out the contents of their nose in the street. This is acceptable behaviour but the Chinese consider it to be extremely vulgar to blow the nose on a handkerchief then replace this in a pocket.

CHOCOLATE

Before their chest was cut open so their heart could be ripped out Aztec sacrifice victims were treated to a cup of hot chocolate.

When Swedish chocolate salesman Roland Ohisson died in 1973 he was buried in a coffin made from chocolate.

Kit Kat was originally an 18th century mutton pie.

The richest man in Italy (2017) is Michele Ferrero. His chocolate lines include Ferrero Rocher, Kinder Eggs, Mon Cheri and Nutella.

In a 2013 online survey 71% of the women who took part said they preferred chocolate to sex.

Ruth Graves Wakefield invented the chocolate chip cookie in 1938. The original name for the biscuit was 'The Toll House Cookie.' She gave the recipe to Nestle for one dollar plus a lifetime supply of their chocolate.

Chocolate affects the heart and nervous system of dogs. Just a few ounces is enough to kill smaller dogs.

As well as the famous Chocolate Orange, Terry's used to make a Chocolate Apple and a Chocolate Lemon.

CITY STATUS

It is a commonly held fallacy that a city must have a cathedral. At the time of writing in 2017 there are 18 British cities with no Anglican or Scottish Episcopal cathedral and 13 towns plus one village with either an Anglican or Scottish Episcopal cathedral but no city status. (Note: Countless books and websites give different statistics for towns with cathedrals and for cities without. Confusion arises due to the requirements for city status having been changed through the years and, in several cases, cities losing their status which some later regained. The figures given here were reached after researching details supplied by the individual towns and cities). (See References)

Cities without cathedrals:

Bath, Brighton and Hove, Cambridge, Hull, Lancaster, Leeds, Newry, Nottingham, Plymouth, Preston, Salford, Southampton, Stirling, Sunderland, Stoke, Swansea, Westminster, Wolverhampton.

Towns with cathedrals:

Blackburn, Brecon, Bury St Edmunds, Guildford, Rochester, Southwark, Southwell, Ayr, Motherwell, Paisley, Clogher, Downpatrick, Dromore and Enniskillen.

The one thing a city must have to officially call itself a city is a Royal Charter.

Ripon is officially the oldest city in Britain with a charter dating back to 886.

CIVET

Perfume manufacturers use a musk obtained from the anal glands of the African civet cat.

The world's most expensive coffee, Kopi Luwak alternatively known as fox-dung coffee or civet coffee, is prepared using coffee cherries that have passed through the digestive system of the Asian palm civet.

The flesh of the coffee cherry is digested by the civet whilst the bean is passed after enzymes within the stomach have given the beans their prized flavour and aroma.

There is a campaign encouraging coffee drinkers to buy only ethical civet coffee since it was revealed the animals are kept in tiny cages in Vietnam where they are force-fed the coffee cherries.

In the interests of research the author taste-tested civet coffee and found little, if any, difference from good quality normal coffee.

COLOURFUL

Several global marketing companies carried out a survey to find the world's favourite colour. Blue came top with 40% approval. Purple, red and green were almost together in second place with yellow, white and orange being least popular.

Lime is always green on a paint colour chart but ripe limes are yellow.

Tests prove that hot chocolate tastes better from a cream or orange cup.

Babies start to see in colour at about the age of two weeks. Red is the first colour they see due to it having a longer wavelength.

Pink is soothing which is why some prisons have pink painted cells to discourage inmates from fighting.

'Khaki' is the Urdu word for 'dust.'

Scientists say red and yellow can make you feel hungry. Interesting to note McDonald's, Pizza Hut and Wimpy all have red and yellow logos.

In Paris the McDonald's 'Golden Arches' are white because the city authorities think the usual yellow is tasteless.

Although the Irish refer to Guinness as 'The Black Stuff'. Guinness is actually very dark red. (See Ale and Hearty)

Yellow is rarely seen in aircraft cabin colour schemes as this colour can make you dizzy. Yellow is also considered to be the most irritating of all colours due to its excessive stimulation of the eyes.

On average, white cars are involved in the least number of accidents with silver coming a close second.

Blue paint was once so expensive that artists only ever used it for the robes of Jesus and Mary.

The ancient Egyptians had a colour called 'Mummy'. Mummy paint, a shade of brown, was actually made from ground-up mummies.

COMETS

In 1910 there was international panic when the Earth passed through the tail of Halley's Comet. Although there was no physical evidence to be seen of the tail it was reported in the press that a gas called cyanogen had been discovered in our atmosphere and this led to fears that everyone would be poisoned. Entrepreneurs made a fortune selling gas masks and anti-comet pills.

The word 'comet' comes from a Greek word meaning long-haired star.

The main body of a comet, the nucleus, consists of ice, gases and dust. The tail appears when heat from the Sun blows ice crystals and dust away. Although, when viewed from Earth, the body of a comet might look as though it is travelling at the front dragging the tail behind it, the tail always points away from the Sun so it can, in fact, be in front of the nucleus.

Annual meteor showers are caused by dust from the tails of long-gone comets.

COMPUTERS

At the start of 2017 it was reported almost half of British children could use a tablet before they could speak.

Apple, Hewlett Packard and Microsoft all started business in garages.

From 1962 to 1973 the computer launch code for US nuclear missiles was 00000000.

A modern mobile phone has much more power than all the computers employed to take the Apollo 11 crew to the Moon.

A 16th century word for 'enamel' was 'email.'

While using a computer the blink-rate drops to around seven times per minute. The average blink-rate is twenty times per minute.

'Password' is one of the most commonly used passwords due to people literally following the instruction, 'Type 'password' here.'

CRITICS

'A critic is someone who knows the way but can't drive the car.' — Kenneth Tynan

'I love criticism just so long as it's unqualified praise.' — Noel Coward

'You can't please everybody. Don't let criticism worry you.' — Robert Louis Stevenson

'It ain't what they call you, it's what you answer to.' — W.C. Fields (See W.C.)

CUSTOMS

Tankanakuy is an event held annually on 25th December in Chumbivilcas Province, near Cuzco in Peru and has now spread to several other villages. The festival includes dancing but the main event involves individuals fighting to settle old conflicts. Once the winners have been established everyone drinks and dances together and they begin the New Year with a clean slate.

November 25th is St Catherine's Day. In France this is celebrated by requiring all unmarried women aged 25 to spend the day wearing green and yellow hats.

Unmarried 25-year-old Germans are expected to celebrate their birthday by following a garland of tied-together socks from their home to the party venue. Drinking along the way is actively encouraged .

In the Czech Republic men go from house to house on Easter Monday lightly whipping women with braided willow branches. This is said to encourage fertility.

Every year the Finish town of Sonkajarvi hosts the World Wife Carrying Championships.

In the Netherlands it is traditional to congratulate the entire family when it's someone's birthday.

In the ancient Persian Empire it was customary for men to debate ideas twice, once when sober and then again when drunk. If the idea sounded okay in both states it was considered to be good.

DANCE

Until 2016 spontaneous dancing was illegal in Sweden except in premises with a dance licence.

Indian cave paintings dating back 9,000 years are the oldest evidence of dancing.

Although Johann Strauss is usually given credit for inventing the waltz in the 19th century, the dance can be traced back to the 16th century.

The waltz was originally performed with couples at arm's length. The close embrace became popular when Queen Victoria took up the dance.

Prior to becoming an international rap star, Tupac Shakur was a ballet dancer. (See Hair)

In 1518, the Dancing Plague was a mania that lasted for a month and killed dozens of people in Strasbourg, France through exhaustion or heart attacks. People danced uncontrollably until they collapsed. (See Mass Hysteria)

DANGEROUS STATISTICS

'People come up with statistics to prove anything. 14% of people know that.' — Homer Simpson (See Homer Simpson - The Wit and Wisdom)

A 2005 survey found that one in five people admitted to having taken a drug called Derbisol. No such drug exists.

Let us take a look at statistics concerning one sport, boxing.

There are those who want boxing banned and vociferous enthusiasts of the sport. Both factions produce statistics to support their claims.

Interestingly neither faction supply dates for their statistics so they may, or may not, be comparable.

Neurosurgeon John Gleave carried out twelve years research to come up with the statistic that, so far as head injuries are concerned, boxing is forty times safer than horse riding.

Anti-boxers tell us that since the Marquis of Queensbury's Rules were introduced in 1884 there have been more than 500 deaths in the ring.

At the time of writing, the World Boxing Council's most recent report of a death was when its President Elect, Jose Sulaiman, died at the age of 85 in 2014. Their records claim 317 boxers have died of injuries sustained in the ring since 1945 but fail to report when the last of these deaths occurred so there could have been a further 317 since.

One actual date I discovered for myself is that 22 died as a result of boxing injuries in 1953.

Undated US Department of Health statistics are quoted by pro-boxers. These do not correlate the number of people taking part in a sport with the number of deaths nor are we given the period over which the statistics were gathered. This is said to show the annual number of deaths attributed to each activity.

Scuba diving   1,100
Skydiving   370
Mountaineering   308
Hang gliding   169
Motorcycle racing   77
Auto racing   34
Horse racing   23
Boxing   10

I'm sure any statistician reading this will be able to prove that boxing should be banned … or should not be banned.

DATING

A struggling cafe owner in China relaunched his business by placing lonely hearts adverts on the internet and fixing for all the potential daters to meet in his cafe.

Most relationships break up in the period between three and five months.

A poll published by Elle magazine revealed that 31% of men dumped a partner they'd found online when she turned out to be overweight. This compares with only 12% of women who made the same claim.

Although beautiful looking women receive more admiring glances and complimentary comments than average-looking women, they are often easier to date as the average guy is intimidated to ask them so they get less invitations to go out.

Almost 50 million people in the US have tried online dating.

The biggest turn-off in a first date is bad breath and the biggest turn-on is the regular use of the other person's name in conversation.

The average man is likely to say he's fallen in love after three dates, the average woman won't say the same thing until date 14.

Speed Dating was launched in 1999 by a rabbi. It is based on the tradition of chaperoned get-togethers for Jewish singles.

A 2015 survey listed the worst places to go on a first date. In order these were: Fast food restaurants, your child's birthday party or school play, your parents' house, a strip club or X-rated movie, swingers party, any event where your ex partner will be present, church activity, window shopping.

Internet dating sites reveal that women who post a photo receive twice as many messages as women who don't. Men claiming an income of $250,000+ receive 156% more emails than those with $50,000 or less.

DEADLY

Manfredo Settela who died in 1680 is the only person in recorded history to have been killed by a falling meteorite.

You are more likely to be killed by a coconut falling from a tree than from a shark attack.

In an average year sharks kill twelve people. In an average year people kill 11,417 sharks.

More than 200 dead bodies serve as landmarks on the slopes of Mount Everest.

On your next birthday around 153,000 people will die.

The oldest person in the World dies every eight months on average.

A company in Georgia, USA, specialises in mixing your loved one's ashes with cement then dropping this into the ocean to become part of a coral reef.

On average left-handed people die three years earlier than right-handed people.

The company LifeGem will turn your loved one's ashes into a diamond.

The last sense to go as you are dying is hearing.

Before Donald Trump suggested banning immigrants to save Americans from terrorist attacks he should have checked the facts. In 2014 more Americans died after slipping in their bathtubs or being struck by lightning than in terrorist attacks.

DESERTS

The Dungeness Nature Reserve in Kent, UK, claims to be classed as a desert due to its low rainfall. A call to the Met Office revealed that they refute this claim but, considering their record for accurate weather forecasts, who do we believe?

The only country in Africa or the Middle East with no desert is Lebanon.

Despite what anyone else tells you, the Sahara is not the world's largest desert. The world's largest desert is Antarctica.

The whole of the USA would fit into the Sahara Desert with space left over.

Due to lack of humidity the temperature in most deserts plunges below freezing in the winter.

DING DONG

The Columbian Liberty Bell was manufactured from metal donations received from over 200,000 patriotic people. Items used in the bell included wedding rings, brooches, watches, Thomas Jefferson's kettle, George Washington's surveying chain plus many other metal objects of historical and sentimental value.

The 7-foot-tall bell was rung at the Columbian Exposition on the Fourth of July 1893 and it was then to become the symbol of peace for the Daughters of the American Revolution.

When the exposition closed the massive bell was found to be missing and it still hasn't been found.

Big Ben isn't a clock and it isn't a tower. Big Ben is the bell that bongs the hour. Until 2012 the famous tower was known as the Clock Tower, it was renamed the Elizabeth Tower to celebrate the Diamond Jubilee in 2012. In 2017 Big Ben stopped bonging, except on special occasions, for four years due to a repair and cleaning programme.

DISASTERS

The story of the world's first air disaster began in the U.K. when a vast R101 airship took flight in October 1930.

Lord Thomson, the Air Minister, rushed through the launch of the R101 despite the required technology still being in its infancy. He wanted to make a spectacular arrival in India for the first Imperial Conference.

Some 3,000 people witnessed the largest flying object ever built in Britain as it departed from Cardington, Bedfordshire and thousands more waved and cheered as she passed overhead.

54 passengers were on board including Lord Thomson. During the afternoon of the following day the weather suddenly deteriorated and the last call from the airship was an enquiry about her location.

The lost dirigible hit a hillside in France and immediately burst into flames. Only eight people survived the crash and two of these died shortly afterwards.

In 2012 there were 905 major natural catastrophes including severe storms, droughts, earthquakes, tornadoes, floods, typhoons, hail storms, hurricanes and wildfires.

Floods in Australia in 2010/11 caused the level of the world's seas to fall by seven millimetres. This was due to there only being a constant quantity of water on the Earth, whether in the form of liquid, ice or vapour. Huge quantities of water remaining on the land surface, as in flooding, obviously lower the level of the oceans.

The London Symphony Orchestra were booked to sail on the Titanic's maiden voyage but changed ships at the last minute.

More than half the victims of Hurricane Katrina and Hurricane Sandy were over the age of 65.

The three deadliest natural disasters were all in China:

July 1931. Flooding killed between 1,000,000 and 4,000,000.

September 1887. The Yellow River flooded killing between 900,000 and 2,000,000.

January 1556. The Shaanxi earthquake killed an estimated 830,000.

The discrepancy between the highest and lowest possible number of victims is due to different sources giving different figures across the years. They blame this on the huge area covered by these disasters and the fact many victims' bodies were never recovered.

The 1918 flu pandemic killed more than 20 million people worldwide but is never listed as a natural disaster.

It is even more difficult to find accurate details of casualties in man- made disasters due to governments not always admitting to how many died and to many such disasters having knock-on effects. People dying after the initial disaster and, in the case of nuclear disasters, victims dying later from related cancers.

Some of the major man made disasters include:

1952. The London Smog. Recent research has put the number of prematures deaths as 12,000.

1986. Chernobyl Disaster. The original, official death toll, at what is considered the worst nuclear disaster in history, was just two. Later in the year this was upped to 31. A United Nations study estimated the total of premature deaths associated with Chernobyl at 4,000.

1984. Union Carbide India Ltd, Bhopal. More than half a million people were exposed to methyl isocyanate gas and other toxic chemicals. The leak claimed the lives of 2,259 people.

DIVORCE

From 1920 to 1983 leprosy was grounds for divorce in Greece.

Divorce is still illegal in the Philippines and the Vatican City. Divorce was illegal in Malta until a referendum in 2011.

In the USA the average divorced woman waits 3.1 years before remarrying, the average man waits 3.3 years.

There is a 75% chance of a marriage breaking up if only one partner smokes.

A 2013 survey in the UK showed that 50% of divorcees regretted getting divorced.

Jewish law once gave a man permission to divorce his wife if she 'found no favour in his eyes because he hath found some uncleanliness in her.'

In 2012 an Italian woman applied for a divorce on the grounds that her husband had taken his mother on their honeymoon.

If a man mistreats his mother-in-law this is not grounds for divorce in Wichita, Kansas.

In New York and Mississippi a spouse is allowed to sue a third-party for being responsible for a marriage failure. The case is known as 'alienation of affection.'

Marriages where the woman is two or more years older than the man are 55% more likely to break up than marriages where the man is two or more years older than the woman.

Two-thirds of divorce applications in Italy in 2016 mentioned the apps WhatsApp or Facebook. Facebook was mentioned in a third of UK divorces in 2015.

A 1943 survey in the UK came up with the unpredicted fact that to avoid divorce you had to like your partner.

DOME SWEET DOME

Domes are the most efficient form of construction, being lighter, stronger and using less material than any other type of structure.

Ely Cathedral boasts the world's only Gothic dome.

The Pantheon in Rome is thought to have been dedicated in 126 AD and is recognised as the most perfectly preserved ancient Roman building thanks to its continuous use.

Few visitors realise the huge dome, with a hole in the middle that lets the rain pour in, is constructed from concrete. With a diameter of 43 metres it is the largest unreinforced concrete dome in the world.

The London Millennium Dome (Now the O2 Arena) and the Eden Project were record breakers in their time.

DOVES OF PEACE (OR SHOULD THAT BE PIECES OF DOVES?)

Three doves are said to represent the Holy Trinity so it has long been a custom to release doves at weddings, funerals and national events.

Doves operate like homing pigeons so they are not actually being set free, they head straight home but they don't always make it.

A trio of doves went viral on the internet in 2017 when they were filmed being released by mourners at a funeral in the USA and two of them flew straight into a fast moving truck on a nearby highway.

Apartheid's peace-making affect on South Africa was celebrated in May 1960 at a rally during which apartheid architect Dr Verwoerd tossed a symbolic white dove of peace above the heads of the crowd. The dove flapped to the ground, refusing to fly, and was rescued by an onlooker.

A whole host of doves were released during the opening ceremony of the Seoul Olympics in 1988. Instead of heading straight home many sat around the rim of a large bowl to watch the rest of the exciting event. Unfortunately the bowl around which they had settled quickly became an inferno as the Olympic Flame was ignited and roosting became roasting

There is apparently no truth in reports that barbecued doves were served at corporate events as canapés.

DRINK

'You're not drunk if you can lie on the floor without holding on.' — Dean Martin

'I'm sorry the show has been delayed but the drummer has been taken suddenly drunk.' — Ronnie Scott, jazz musician and club owner.

Gioacchino Antonio Rossini could only compose when seriously inebriated and wrapped in blankets.

It is claimed that if you feed alcohol to an ant and it will eventually fall over on its righthand side.

The wire cage that holds a champagne cork in place is called a muselet.

More than 30% of bread produced in the UK is thrown away but only 6% of alcohol.

It takes approximately 700 grapes to make one bottle of wine.

It is a fact that the last part of the body to be cleared of alcohol is the brain.

A 2012 survey revealed that diners buy more expensive wines if a restaurant plays classical music.

The above survey also found that diners poured 12% more wine into a handheld glass than they did into one standing on the table.

The only proven cure for a hangover is more alcohol. Preferably something fizzy to take the alcohol swiftly to the bloodstream.

Ever helpful Russian scientists have developed a drug that prolongs the affects of drunkenness.

Water to brew Guinness is piped from the Wicklow Mountains. Despite the brewery being close to the River Liffey and the drink being known as 'Liffey Water' it contains no water from the river.

Guinness was the first drink with a widget in its can.

Fockink Gin comes from Holland.

Drinks you are unlikely to find in your local pub or restaurant include; Baby Mouse Wine, Elephant Dung Beer, Snake Wine, Urine Whisky, Whale Testicle Beer and Three Penis Rice Wine.

Braggers who claim to have drunk Tequila with a worm in it are wrong on both counts. It isn't Tequila and it isn't a worm. The drink Mezcal contains a moth larva.

Mojito derives from mojadito, Spanish for 'a little wet'.

E

eBAY

It is claimed eBay was originally set up for collectors to trade Pez dispensers. This has been refuted as a PR stunt. Pez dispensers were traded on eBay in its early days but this was not the purpose for setting it up.

An early item sold on eBay was a broken laser pointer for $22.40. eBay creator, Pierre Omidyar, sent an email to the purchaser to ask if he realised it was broken and the man replied, 'I'm a collector of broken laser pointers.'

Although eBay began in America it was the British who made most purchases per capita in 2016.

In 2012 Buford, a town in Wyoming, was sold on eBay to Vietnamese buyers for $900,000.

Singer James Blunt claims to have auctioned his sister on eBay. Before he was rich and famous, he arrived home to find her crying because she could not get to a funeral in Ireland as planes were on strike and it was out of season for ferries. Blunt advertised the 'Damsel in Distress' on eBay and the highest bidder was a man with a helicopter. Three years later the duo were married.

Towards the end of its active life the Space Shuttle was kept operating with obsolete technology such as floppy disks and Intel 8086 chips purchased by NASA via eBay.

ECLIPTIC

Emperor Louis of Bavaria died of fright in AD840 at the sight of a solar eclipse.

The 1961 movie 'Barabbas' was almost awarded an Academy Award for Special Effects. Just in time someone pointed out to the judges that the crucifixion scene had been filmed against the background of an actual total eclipse of the Sun.

The Golden Jubilee Test between India and England in 1980 is the only major sporting event to have been officially interrupted by an eclipse of the Sun. The Indian Cricket Board didn't want to be responsible for damage to 50,000 pairs of eyes as spectators viewed the eclipse so the match was cancelled for the day, enabling 50,000 spectators to damage their eyes in the comfort of their own back yards.

During a total solar eclipse the Moon's shadow, known as the umbra, travels across the Earth at varying speeds. Due to the Earth's shape the 2017 eclipse that crossed the USA saw the Moon's shadow travelling at around 1,500 mph at the centre of its path and approximately one thousand miles faster at the ends.

Total solar eclipses occur because, by pure chance. The Sun is 400 times larger than the Moon and is also 400 times further from the earth. This makes the two bodies appear to be the same size in our sky.

EDUCATION

Wikipedia Zero offers all the facts on Wikipedia with no roaming charges to mobile phone users in 34 poor countries.

12% of the world's adults are considered to be functionally illiterate.

George Lucas sold Lucasfilm Ltd to Disney for $4.05 billion and donated the entire proceeds to a charity supporting education.

ELECTIONS

'I never vote for anyone. I always vote against.' — W.C. Fields (See W.C.)

Americans vote on a Tuesday, Australians and New Zealanders on Saturday and Brits vote on a Thursday but most people around the world vote on Sundays.

It is compulsory to vote in Australia. Failure to vote carries a fine of AU$20 increasing to AU$180 for failure to pay and possible criminal charges.

The busiest polling station in Australian elections is in London, England with over 15,000 votes cast there.

Despite the above, Belgium is ranked as the country with the largest percentage of voters with a 87.2% turnout in 2016.

In 1967 the town of Piacoaza in Ecuador elected a foot deodorant as town mayor.

India is the world's largest democracy with 800 million eligible voters. The 2014 Indian election took place on nine different days over a period of five weeks.

So many people in the Gambia are illiterate they vote by selecting a marble with a picture of their chosen candidate and then dropping this into a box. Each marble rings a bell so officials know if they hear two dings someone has cheated.

In 2005 Estonia became the first country to offer online voting. An ID card and PIN confirm identity, anonymity is maintained because votes are encrypted.

Another one of those 'facts' on which there is much confusion is the eligibility for the British Monarch to vote. The Monarch has a vote just the same as everyone else but usually does not exercise this right.

ELEMENTARY

Sherlock Holmes does not say 'Elementary my dear Watson,' in any of Conan Doyle's books. Neither does he wear a deerstalker hat or smoke a calabash pipe.

Sir Arthur Conan Doyle's first novel was never published. His only manuscript was lost in the post.

Sherlock Holmes had only one girlfriend. Irene Adler appears in one story, 'A Scandal in Bohemia' and she never sees the famous sleuth as himself. On their only meetings he is in disguise either as a clergyman or a drunk.

Sherlock Holmes is the most-portrayed literary human character on film and television (Hamlet comes second). IMDB lists Holmes as having appeared in 292 movies and TV shows.

ELVIS

Elvis is Norse for 'all wise.'

Elvis never performed abroad because his manager, the self-styled 'Colonel', Tom Parker, was an illegal immigrant and afraid if he went outside the US he wouldn't be allowed back in.

At the age of ten Elvis came fifth in a talent contest singing 'Old Shep.'

Elvis purchased the 23-room mansion Graceland when he was 22-years-old. It overlooks Route 51, now named Elvis Presley Boulevard.

'Blue' occurs in the titles of 15 songs recorded by Elvis.

Elvis fell in love with future wife Priscilla when she was a fourteen-year-old schoolgirl.

Elvis hated fish and would not allow Priscilla to have it cooked at Graceland.

Between filming 'Love Me Tender' in 1956 and 'Loving You' in 1957 Elvis had his nose fixed, his teeth capped and treatment for acne.

Elvis dyed his naturally blond hair with 'Miss Clairol 51D Black Velvet.'

In each city where he performed Elvis liked to collect a badge from the local police force.

Elvis had a pet turkey named Bowtie.

ENGLISH IN OTHER LANGUAGES

Germans call birth control pills 'antibabypille.' The German name for a mobile phone is a 'Handy.'

Much of the English language was adapted from the Romans but modern Italians have started borrowing back. 'Footing' means jogging, 'autostop' is hitch-hiking and 'flipper' is a pinball machine.

A commercial on Italian TV is known as a 'spot' and traffic is 'il traffico.'

The French claim to have rejected Franglais terms but still have quite a few words and phrases relying heavily on things heard across the English Channel. Of course they never refer to the English Channel ('La Manche' meaning 'The Sleeve') but what about: 'le parking' - car park, 'le weekend' - the weekend, 'les jeans' - jeans, 'le pullover' - pullover or sweater.

In Luxembourgish the response on being asked 'How are you?' is 'Tip Top.'

The Chilean word for 'plumber' is 'gasfiter'.

If you move each letter in the word 'yes' sixteen places along in the alphabet you get 'oui.'

In Japan many youth products such as T-shirts are printed with virtually meaningless slogans in English.

A Japanese white-collar worker is a 'salaryman' an office lady is an 'O.L.' and a Job Centre is 'Hello Work.'

EPITAPHS

Spike Milligan, during one of his many telephone calls to me (see Award Ceremonies), confirmed the well publicised rumour, that he wanted his epitaph to read: 'I told you I was ill.' In a 2012 national survey this was voted Britain's favourite epitaph even though it was never carved on his tombstone. Sussex authorities displayed a sense of humour by-pass by refusing to permit the epitaph in English so Spike's requested epitaph is sculpted in Irish, 'Dúirt mé leat go raibh mé breoite'.

George Spencer Milett worked in a New York insurance company. On his fifteenth birthday in 1909 the girls in the office said that at the end of the working day they would each kiss him once for every year of his life.

The epitaph on his tombstone explains what happened: 'Lost life after falling on an ink eraser evading six young women trying to give him birthday kisses in office Metropolitan Life Building.'

The tombstone of Dee Dee Ramone, of the Ramones rock band, reads: 'O.K...I gotta go now.'

EROS

Every day thousands of tourists from all over Britain and around the world flock to London's Piccadilly Circus to admire the Shaftesbury Memorial Fountain.

Many are aware that this is a rare piece of art as it is cast in aluminium but very few are aware that it is not a statue of Eros.

The famed attraction is actually a statue of Eros' twin brother Anteros. Sculptor Albert Gilbert chose Anteros for the memorial because he believed he represented reflective and mature love, as opposed to Eros who he viewed as frivolous.

ETIQUETTE

The usual seating plan for weddings is groom's family and friends on the right, those of the bride on the left. If members of the Royal Family accept an invitation to attend your nuptials they must be seated on the righthand side of the church or registry office no matter who their friend is.

If you are invited to a royal banquet the signal to start eating is when the Queen unfolds her napkin. If you pop out to the loo you should leave your napkin on your chair.

It is polite to cover your mouth when you cough or sneeze but you should never do this with your right hand. The right hand is the social hand and nobody wants to shake it if it has just been coughed or sneezed into.

It is considered impolite to applaud in front of your own face, even worse to clap in front of someone else's. The polite way to show your appreciation for a performance is to clap the hands slightly to your left at chest height.

If you raise your glass to drink a toast with an Austrian it is seen as the height of bad manners not to look them in the eye.

When drinking a toast in Russia your glass should be raised throughout the toast.

French diners believe the hands should be kept above the table throughout a meal.

In Britain forks are always presented with their prongs (tines) upwards. In France they are usually presented with the prongs down to the table.

If you take someone a gift in Thailand it is traditional to leave the price on.

EXCLAMATION MARK!

Pedants on Facebook regularly moan about friends using one or more exclamation marks after just about anything!

! first appeared in J. Day's 'The Catechism of Edward VI' circa 1553.

So there!

EXECUTIONS

John (Babbacombe) Lee was arrested in 1884 for the murder of Emma Keyse who had been one of Queen Victoria's maids. The murder took place in Babbacombe, Torquay. Lee was found guilty and sentenced to hang.

Hangman James Berry prepared Lee for his meeting with his maker and it is now common knowledge that Lee's sentence was commuted to life imprisonment after Berry's unsuccessful attempt to get the trapdoor to open beneath the condemned man.

Berry's own diaries tell us that two attempts were made to hang Lee but legend maintains there were three attempts. Inspired by this story, folk/rock band Fairport Convention released an album titled 'Babbacombe Lee'.

Other Berry hangings include those of a murderer whose head was ripped off due to too much rope being allowed and another occasion when insufficient rope was used and Berry had to swing on the prisoner's legs to encourage him to die.

Guillotines were not invented by Dr Joseph Guillotin. He had the dubious privilege of having the killing machine named after him because he suggested it would be a humane way of dispatching criminals. The final execution using a guillotine in France took place in 1977.

As early as the 16th century, Halifax in Yorkshire had a gibbet that operated just like the much later guillotine. The Halifax gibbet was used to execute anyone stealing an item worth more than 13 pence. If an animal had been stolen it was attached to the rope that pulled out the pin releasing the blade, thus executing the person who had stolen it. A reconstruction of this device can still be seen in Halifax in the appropriately-named Gibbet Street.

Joe Arridy was known as the happiest man on Death Row. He had an IQ of only 40 and had been coerced into confessing to the rape and murder of a fifteen-year-old girl. He spent his time on Death Row in a Colorado jail playing with a toy train given to him by his guards. For his final meal in 1939 he requested ice-cream and is said to have smiled as he held a warder's hand on his way to the gas chamber, unaware he was about to die.

Emperor Menelik II of Ethiopia said it would help stamp out his country's high crime rate when he purchased three of the recently invented electric chairs from the USA.

Their effectiveness at crime reduction was never tested as Ethiopia had no electricity.

In 2014 the most executions were carried out in China, followed in order by Iran, Iraq, Saudi Arabia and the USA.

The four leading execution countries listed above do not admit to an official number of executions. The USA admitted to 35 in 2014, considerably down on the 98 executions in 1999.

The average victim of execution in the US during 2014 had spent twenty years on death row. Thomas Knight was executed in Florida at the age of 62 after spending 39 years in a cell. The average age of executed offenders at the time of their crime was 28 and their age at execution was 48.

Amnesty International's 2012 report included evidence of one man crucified then beheaded in Saudi Arabia.

In 2012 it is estimated that several thousand criminals were executed in China. The official figure for the rest of the world was 682.

In 2012 21 countries carried out the death penalty.

In 2017 Arkansas announced it would carry out eight executions in eleven days. It went ahead with four of these. The reason for the rushed back-to-back executions was that one of the drugs used for lethal-injections were approaching their use-by date and the British manufacturer refused to supply more.

One of the four drugs injected into US execution victims is only used to paralyse them. This could well prolong and hide their suffering but it makes them look peaceful, so less stressful for onlookers.

If oxygen is completely cut off but a full nitrogen supply maintained nitrogen asphyxiation occurs. The body does not experience any sensation of suffocation and death is painless. No government is known to have ever used this method for capital punishment.

EXTRAS

At the age of 15 Lady Gaga had a bit part in 'The Sopranos'.

John Wayne was an extra in several silent movies before being given his first starring role in 'The Big Trail'.

The guy who says one line, ' The guy's a professional,' in Dean Martin and Jerry Lewis' 1951 comedy 'Sailor Beware' is James Dean.

Brad Pitt was paid $38 for his role as a partygoer in 'Less Than Zero'.

Bruce Willis is easy to spot as an extra in the court scene of Paul Newman's 'The Verdict', 1981.

In 1971 Sylvester Stallone was an extra in Woody Allen's 'Bananas'. He played a subway mugger. In the same year Stallone was an uncredited disco patron in Jane Fonda's 'Klute'.

Ben Affleck and Matt Damon are extras in the 'Field of Dreams' Fenway Park scene.

'Dazed and Confused' sees a group of students including a young Renée Zellweger.

A dancer in the 'Bad Boys 2' club scene is Megan Fox.

F

FADS AND FASHION

People in North Korea must select hair styles from a government approved list of 28.

L.A. Gear reportedly threatened to sue Michael Jackson when he refused to wear their trainers while being paid to make a commercial for them.

In 1947 there was a fad in American colleges for shoe swapping.

Despite being the height of fashion, Hot Pants were banned from the Royal Enclosure at Ascot in 1971.

There is no law in the USA preventing lipstick from containing arsenic, lead and mercury.

What was once a size-8 dress can now be bought as size-0 thanks to what is known as 'vanity sizing'.

'Conversesjukan' is a Swedish word meaning foot problems caused by wearing trainers. (See Foreign Phrases)

Clothes manufactured in Saipan sweatshops can legally be sold with 'Made in the USA' labels because Saipan is a US territory.

'Made in America' labels on garments actually made in Saipan include those from Gap, Tommy Hilfiger and Ralph Lauren. (See Urban Myths)

The nominal body weight between two adjacent dress sizes if fifteen pounds.

Heidi Klum was once among the most glamorous models on the planet. She now has her own range of orthopaedic sandals.

Louis XIV brought in a law permitting only members of the royal court to wear red heels.

Women were banned from wearing flat-heeled shoes at gala screenings during the 2015 Cannes Film Festival.

I was 1988 before a model was first seen wearing denim jeans on the cover of Vogue.

There were originally no military-related sets of Lego because the inventor was a pacifist.

The Ann Summers adult store group was founded by a man, Michael Caborn-Waterfield, who named the company after his secretary Annice Summers.

Mini skirt pioneer Mary Quant once observed: 'A woman is as old as her knees.'

Dr Martens boots originally had soles made from recycled car tyres.

Before becoming a popular after shave lotion Old Spice was launched in 1937 as a perfume for women.

The heavily scented patchouli oil, beloved by hippies, is obtained from a member of the mint family.

Until 2007 the Russian military were not supplied with socks.

A designer logo is more essential to some people than the actual style or quality of their clothes. The first such logo was the Lacoste crocodile - and it is a crocodile, not an alligator.

In the 1970s a fortune was made by a company marketing rocks as low maintenance pets.

Americans call a waistcoat a vest.

Singer Katy Perry has a perfume range that includes 'Meow!' and 'Killer Queen'.

During a 2010 visit to the White House, Prime Minister's wife Samantha Cameron presented each of Barack Obama's daughters with a pair of Hunter Wellington boots.

FAILED ATTEMPTS

Sarah Henley jumped from the 250-foot high Clifton Suspension Bridge in 1885. Her crinoline dress opened up like a parachute and gently floated her safely into the Avon gorge.

An Iranian attempt to get into 'The Guinness Book of World Records' by constructing the world's largest sandwich failed when spectators started eating the sandwich before it was finished.

FASCINATING FACTS

Crusaders boiled their dead comrades until the flesh fell away and then took the bones home for Christian burial.

The Dead Sea is a lake.

Potholes take their name from 18th century British potters who would dig holes in the middle of roads to search for clay.

People are twice as likely to believe something they read if it is in bold print.

The saying 'dead as a dodo' comes from a large bird that became extinct in 1681. The only artist known to have painted a dodo from life was Roelandt Savery who wasn't famous for his accuracy. Future generations of artists have used Savery's work as their model which is why most paintings of dodos show the bird with two right legs.

If all of the movies featuring the Pony Express were played end to end they would last much longer than the twelve months (1860 to 1861) during which the actual Pony Express existed.

The only country named after a woman is St Lucia.

It was estimated in 2014 that British councils spend an annual £40,000 removing traffic cones from the heads of statues, mostly close to colleges and universities.

After they have been sheared sheep don't recognise one another and have to re-establish hierarchy by fighting for superiority.

The Boy Scouts 'Be Prepared' motto was originally 'Be Prepared to Die For Your Country.'

Most burns suffered by fire fighters are due to sweat boiling on their skin.

A county councillor in Staffordshire, England, used civic funds to purchase a police speed camera. Shortly after installation one of the camera's first victims was the councillor.

A Ugandan woman gave birth to a baby on a flight from Amsterdam to Boston. The baby was declared to be Canadian as it was born in Canadian airspace.

Before refrigeration was invented people in Russia kept a frog swimming in their milk. Secretions from the frog's skin inhibited the growth of bacteria.

Martin Luther King Jr was homophobic and believed homosexuality could be cured by psychiatrists.

Aglets are the plastic bits on the ends of shoelaces.

Keepers are the loops through which a belt is run.

Ikea claim that one in ten Europeans was conceived in one of their beds.

ATM PINs were intended to have six digits, but only have four because the inventor's wife said that was all she could remember.

For several years the UK TV commercial for Smarties, chocolate beans, ended with the words; 'How many Smarties would it take to fill Wembley Stadium? Only Smarties have the answer.' With an idea for a Trivial Pursuit question, the author telephoned Rowntrees to ask how many Smarties it would take to fill Wembley Stadium and was told to stop wasting their time.

In Italy there's a school for drag queens

FEET

'I have little feet because nothing grows in the shade.' — Dolly Parton (See Quotable Quotes)

The circumference of an elephant's foot is half the height of the elephant.

It is best to purchase shoes in the afternoon. Feet tend to swell during the day and if they fit in the afternoon they should be okay at any time.

In 2013 there was an exhibition in Dublin of cheeses made with bacteria obtained from feet. (See Cheese)

The feet contain about a quarter of the bones in your body. Each foot has 26 bones.

Your big toes each have two bones, the other toes have three.

A pair of feet has about 250,000 sweat glands and can produce half a pint of sweat per day.

Women have four times more foot problems than men with high heels mostly to blame.

As you walk your toes carry half your body weight each time you lift your heel from the ground.

FINAL THOUGHTS

Phineas T. Barnum of Barnum and Bailey Circus fame — 'How were today's receipts at Madison Square Garden?'

Actor Richard Burton had a standing bet with his brothers

that they would never catch him without at least one item of red clothing to signify his Welsh roots. When he died in 1984 Burton was buried in Switzerland dressed from head to toe in red.

Gareth Jones died in 1958 during a live television performance of the play 'Underground'. The rest of the cast were told to ad lib to make up for the fact they were an actor short and it's doubtful any of the viewers noticed that Jones had gone.

Ben Jonson is buried standing up in Poets' Corner, Westminster Abbey.

D.H. Lawrence's last words are said to have been: 'I think I am getting better.'

Elvis Presley didn't go out with a song. His final words were to his fiancé Ginger Alden who he told, 'I'm going to the bathroom to read.' (See Elvis)

Composer Jean-Philippe Rameau was visited on his deathbed by a priest who began to sing a hymn. Rameau objected to this and his final words were: 'What the devil do you mean to sing to me priest? You are out of tune.'

Margaret Sanger, the birth control pioneer, left this world with the words: 'A party, let's have a party.'

Nostradamus, the seer whose prophecies supposedly predicted everything from the sinking of the Titanic to the rise of Adolf

Hitler, made one final prediction. On 1st July 1566 he went to bed with the words, 'Tomorrow at sunrise I shall no longer be here.' He was right.

Marie Antoinette's final utterance was an apology to her executioner as she stepped on his foot on her way to the guillotine. (See Executions)

Drummer Buddy Rich died in 1987 following surgery. Before he was wheeled into the operating theatre a nurse responsible for drugs asked him if there was anything he couldn't take. He replied: 'Yes, country music.'

It is still the custom in the USA to permit convicted criminal to order one final meal prior to their execution, although they are not permitted a cigarette as this is deemed dangerous.

Murderer Thomas J. Grasso's final words were to complain he had requested canned Spaghetti-Os but 'I got spaghetti and I want the press to know about this.' (See Executions)

Oscar Wilde's reported last words were, 'Either that wallpaper goes or I do.' Wilde said this several weeks prior to his death. He died in severe pain and his final words were a hardly recognisable Catholic prayer.

Einstein spoke his final words in German to a nurse who only spoke English, so nobody has any idea what he said.

FISHY FACTS

'Fish' is the term for a single species even when talking about multiples: e.g. six fish. 'Fishes' is used when referring to multiples of more than one species: e.g. three cod, four salmon and two trout is a total of nine fishes.

After anglerfish have mated, they melt into each other to share bodies for the rest of their lives. When a male finds a female, he connects on and fuses to her, he loses his internal organs until they share a bloodstream.

Most fish have tastebuds all over their bodies. A fish can have up to 27,000 tastebuds, a human has 7,000. (See Human Body)

Starfish and jellyfish aren't fish.

It is cheaper to have Scottish fish sent to China for filleting and then sent back to Scotland than it is to have it filleted where it was caught.

Sharks are the only fish with eyelids.

The Celestial Eye Goldfish really does have eyes bigger than its stomach.

A third of the male fish in British waters change sex to female. This is blamed on human sewage in the water.

FLORAL TRIBUTES

In Russia it is expected that carnations or roses will be presented to the girl on a first date. The bouquet must include an odd number of flowers as even numbers are reserved for funerals.

California grows 60% of the USA's cut-flowers.

In the 17th century tulip bulbs were worth more than gold in Holland.

All parts of a tulip are edible. The bulb can be used as a substitute for onions in cooking but does not have the same flavour.

Marsh marigold buds can be pickled and used as a substitute for capers.

Dandelion flowers and leaves are a good source of vitamins A and C, calcium, iron and potassium.

Bluebell juice was used in early glue.

FLYING HIGH

56% of pilots surveyed in Britain, Norway and Sweden admitted to having fallen asleep in flight and 29% of these said they'd woken up to find their co-pilot asleep.

Flying is the safest form of mass transport. Odds against dying in a road accident are 5,000 to one, odds against dying in an air crash are 11,000 to one.

More deaths occur in accidents involving passengers in taxis on their way to or from the airport than in plane crashes.

Commercial planes are built to fly on one engine. If all engines stop even a large plane can still glide a considerable distance.

There has been a lot of publicity over passengers allegedly becoming ill due to recycled, germ-filled air on planes. Only half the air is recycled and that is filtered 20 to 30 times. The other half is replaced every two or three minutes from a built-in air system. Your home probably has more bacteria in the air than the average passenger jet.

Between 1988 and 2016 an estimated 200 people died in the USA due to airborne collisions between planes and birds.

Finnair operates a regular flight number 666 from Copenhagen to Hel (Helsinki).

In 2013 37-stone Les Prince was told he had to pay for two seats on a flight from Ireland to England. When he arrived at the airport the airline had allocated him seats on different rows of the aircraft.

80% of plane crashes take place in the first three minutes after take-off and the last eight minutes before landing.

The Hindenburg airship was going to be called the Hitler.

FOODY FADS

Brits buy brown eggs, Americans buy white. American eggs would be illegal in the UK and most of Europe, not due to their colour but because they are washed and sanitised. Although this might sound like the American eggs are cleaner, eggs have a very thin outer layer called the cuticle protecting them from contamination. The US washing process removes this protection. This is why American supermarkets keep eggs in the fridge, British eggs do not need refrigeration.

Biscuits in Britain are crunchy, sweet treats, often with a chocolate coating, to be enjoyed with a cup of tea, or savoury snacks to accompany beer. In America biscuits are similar to a plain UK scone, served with breakfast, coated with 'gravy.' The gravy is a white sauce with bits of sausage.

Christmas treats for Eskimo children include mattack. Mattack is whaleskin with a layer of raw blubber on its inside. I confess to having done no research into this delicacy, it apparently tastes like coconut but is so rubbery that it has to be swallowed in lumps.

When the mattack runs out the 'icing on the cake' comes in the form of kiviak. Kiviak is made by packing a sealskin with the raw flesh of awks and then burying this for several months until the whole delightful mess reaches an advanced state of decomposition. If they get the timing right this takes the place of Christmas Pudding at the end of the festive meal.

By the time they leave high school most American children will have eaten 1,500 peanut-butter-and-jelly sandwiches. What Brits know as 'jam' is called 'jelly' in the US. What Brits know as 'jelly' is 'jello' in America, taking it's name from the brand name 'Jell-O.'

Mangoes are members of the same plant family as pistachios and cashews. Some people with nut allergies have the same reaction to mangoes.

In Britain it is polite to eat asparagus with the fingers, in Germany you must use a knife and fork. Brits literally 'break bread' with their hands, in Germany you must use a knife.

Frogs' legs were regularly eaten in Britain some 7,000 years before they were discovered by the French.

Food rationing was brought into operation in Britain in 1940 - one year before the launch of 'Gourmet' magazine in the USA.

'Peppier' is the name given to a waiter whose job is to walk around grinding black pepper on to your dinner.

Prunes didn't sell very well in the USA as people didn't know what they were. Sales took a massive boost when they were relabelled as 'dried plums.'

If you see E175 listed as a food coating this is pure gold.

Weight for weight potatoes have the same amount of calories as apples.

According to his personal chef, late North Korean leader, Kim Jon Il, enjoyed eating hippos, snakes and spiders.

Canadians eat more donuts per capita than any other nationality on Earth.

Donuts are known as Gravy Rings in Ireland.

There is no law against cannibalism in the UK. If that's got you interested a 12.5 stone man (79.4 kilos) has 110,000 calories.

No matter what TV chefs and cooking programme presenters tell you there is no such thing as a restauranteur. There is no N in the word which is restaurateur.

Mrs Beaton recommended that pasta should be boiled for almost two hours.

Greek yoghurt is natural yoghurt with the whey removed.

The Jersey Royal is the only potato with a region of origin name protected by E.U. legislation.

Food rationing ended in Britain in 1954 - one year before those American gourmets launched the McDonald's burger.

McDonald's and Burger King coat their fries with dextrose, a type of sugar, to make them golden when fried.

Food company Heinz's bank balance was somewhat lighter after they paid $71 million for Weight Watchers in 1978.

When asked to confirm the well-documented belief that he was allergic to carrots. Mel Blanc, the voice of Bugs Bunny, said he wasn't allergic to them but did not like them. (See Road Runner)

The first product marketed by Heinz was grated horseradish.

The average price per pound paid for potato crisps (chips in the US) is 200 times more than for the same quantity of potatoes.

Refried Beans are only fried once. In Spanish their name is 'frijoles refritos' which sounds like 'refried' but actually means well-fried'.

President Gerald Ford always ordered the same menu for lunch: cottage cheese with brown sauce and a sliced tomato followed by ice- cream.

A spurtle is an instrument used by Scotsmen to stir their porridge.

A London restaurant introduced Baby Gaga ice-cream in 2012. Advertised as the most expensive ice-cream in the city at £15 per scoop, it contains human breast milk.

Said to be the world's most expensive cheese, Serbian Pule is made from donkey milk.

Queen Victoria enjoyed an Indian curry every Tuesday and Sunday.

More than 100 shapes of pasta are listed alphabetically from 'anelli' to 'ziti'.

The shape of a pretzel is modelled on the crossed arms of a praying child.

A 2013 online survey revealed that only 43% of Americans include any vegetables, other than potatoes, when making home cooked meals.

Frankfurters were invented by the Chinese.

A crudivor is someone who eats only raw food.

Henry I and Alexander Pope both died after eating a surfeit of lampreys. A lamprey is an eel-shaped fish.

John, King of England, died at Swinestead Abbey after consuming a surfeit of peaches, pears and cider?

Veteran actor Jack Nicholson became addicted to baked beans on toast after serving this as a snack to his son, Raymond.

Tipping restaurant staff is considered an insult in Iceland.

The searing headache that sometimes occurs when eating ice-cream is called sphenopalatine ganglioneuralgia.

A Ritz cracker has seven holes.

FOREIGN PHRASES

When posing for a photo Germans don't say 'cheese.' They say 'ameisensheise,' meaning 'ant shit.'

German mothers-to-be don't have a 'bun in the oven,' they have a 'roast dinner in the oven.'

The French for 'lol' is 'mdr' - 'mort de rire' meaning 'dead from laughing.' (See ABC)

The French word for 'sexting' is 'textopornographique.'

The Turkish word for turkey means 'Indian bird.'

The Indian word for turkey means 'Peruvian bird'.

The Inuit word 'iktsuarpok' means that you keep popping outside to see if anyone is coming.

The Norwegian word for smelly feet is 'tafis', meaning 'toe fart.' (See Petomane)

In Germany the noise made by Rice Krispies is 'Knisper! Knasper! Knusper!'

In Japan 'tsundoku' means to keep buying books you are not going to read.

The German phrase, 'Eierlegende Wollmilchsau,' ('egg-laying wool-milk-cow') means a woman who can turn her hand to anything.

The German word for 'losers' is 'Gurkentruppe,' literally meaning an 'army of cucumbers.'

In Spain things don't happen 'when pigs fly,' they happen 'when hens piss.'

FRANCE

The Romans divided France into two halves. 'Hairy Gaul' in the north and 'Trousered Gaul' in the south.

By area France is the third-largest European country after Russia and Ukraine.

France and its overseas departments and territories cover twelve time zones, the most of any country.

French Nobel Literature prize-winner Andre Gide said: 'French people are Italian people in a bad mood.'

France legalised same-sex sexual activity in 1791. The USA took until 2003 to make this same move.

When the Millau Viaduct was completed in 2005 over the Tarn River in the South of France it was the world's tallest bridge. At the time of writing it still is. (See Bridges)

With permission from the President, it is legal in France to marry someone who has died.

It wasn't until 1964 that French women were allowed to open a bank account or obtain a passport without the permission of their husband.

'Le Bon Marche,' which opened in Paris in 1838, was the world's first true department store.

Following a law established in 1798 it was illegal for women in Paris to wear trousers until 2003.

A 2003 survey by the Durex company showed that people in France have sex more often than any other country in the world.

A 2007 survey revealed that the French spend more on medicines than any other country in Europe.

FRUITY

A Westcountry custom required a young man to prick an orange with a fork and sleep with this fruit in his armpit for a night.

The following day he offered the orange to the girl of his dreams and if she ate it she she would be his.

A whole orange will float but it will sink if you peel it.

A kiwi fruit contains double the amount of vitamin C found in an orange.

A strawberry isn't a berry but a banana is.

Strawberries and cashews are the only fruits with their seeds on the outside.

Bananas are a natural antacid and can be used as a cure for heartburn.

Bananas come from the world's largest herb.

The banana is believed to have been the world's first fruit.

Cantaloupe melons can spread bacteria. In 2011, 21 people died in the US due to listeria bacteria in cantaloupes.

The high acid content in lemons makes them good for cleaning thanks to their ability to kill bacteria.

Grapes cannot ripen further once picked, they just rot.

The world's most popular fruit is the tomato.

19th century British sailors were known as Limeys because they ate limes to prevent scurvy.

g

GAMESHOWS

In 2004 FOX TV began a series tastefully titled 'Who's Your Daddy?' In each show a young woman who had been adopted as a child was introduced to eight men. One was her father, the others were fakes. After three rounds of questioning the girl won $50,000 if she correctly identified her father. If she failed the money went to one of the false fathers.

FOX were also the innovators who introduced America to 'Man vs Beast'. People had to compete against animals in assorted events and the animals usually won. Former hot dog eating champion Takeru Kobayashi lost an eating competition against a half-ton bear and, in established Fox disputable taste, 44 dwarfs lost to an elephant in an airplane-pulling race.

'Cash Cab' had a short life in the UK. In the USA and Canada it was more popular . 'Trivial Pursuit' was invented in Canada so anything involving questions and answers was lapped up by TV viewers there.

The 'Cash Cab' format saw competitors picked up by a cab and having to answer trivia questions fired at them by the presenter who was their driver. Correct answers brought them an ever-increasing cash prize but three incorrect answer saw them kicked out of the cab before reaching their destination. They had two help options. Phoning a friend on their mobile or shouting out of the cab window seeking assistance from a total stranger.

The franchise received negative publicity in 2011 when one

of the show's producers ran over and killed a 61-year-old pedestrian in Vancouver as he drove the cab back to its garage.

'The Price is Right' climaxed with the remaining two contestants trying to estimate the value of their 'Showcase' stack of prizes with the one who came closest winning the lot.

In 2008 a contestant on the US version of the show guessed $23,743 which was the exact price of his Showcase that included a camper van, billiards table and karaoke machine.

He hadn't cheated. He watched many shows and realised lots of the prizes were repeatedly featured. After memorising the prices of many items he was lucky when these came up on the day he appeared. His total was $23,000 and when he was asked why he added the final $743 he said this was a total fluke, it was the first three numbers of his bank pin.

'The Price is Right' was cancelled in Brazil after inflation kept making the prices totally wrong by the time each show aired.

A contestant on a US gameshow won the choice between a replica of the Simpsons' house or $75,000. He took the cash.

'Amaan Ramadan' is a TV gameshow screened in Pakistan with prizes for competitors who answer questions about Islam.

The host is Aamir Liaquat Hussain, one of the country's best-known celebrities.

During Ramadan TV shows in the Islamic world fight for ratings and in 2013 Hussain announced what was probably the world's most tasteless gameshow stunt since 'Who's Your Daddy?' The prizes on the show were orphaned babies.

Contestants were pre-vetted to check their suitability as parents and the media in Pakistan praised the shows for saving the lives of abandoned babies.

GAS

The word 'gas' was coined by 17th century Flemish chemist, Jan Baptist van Helmont. It is generally accepted he based this on the Greek word 'chaos' but other sources link 'gas' to 'gast' or 'geist' meaning spirit or ghost.

Liquefied petroleum gas (LPG), purchased in cylinders and used mostly for cooking, is propane or butane. Natural gas piped into houses is mainly methane.

William Murdoch moved from Birmingham to Redruth in 1782 to work for a company manufacturing steam engines for the mining industry. He built an enclosed coal fire in his garden and piped fumes from this into his house where they were ignited to provide illumination. This house displays a plaque declaring it to be the first house in the world with gas lighting..

GEORGE

Saint George is the patron saint of England, Georgia, Malta, Portugal, Romania, Aragon, Catalonia, leprosy and syphilis. According to legend George was a Roman soldier of Greek origin.

Just about anyone who owns a black and white car in Cairo calls himself a taxi driver. It's his job to take tourists to tatty souvenir shops where he receives baksheesh from the shopkeeper. Passengers are encouraged to purchases a recently made 'ancient' relic, a tacky carpet or a 'genuine' papyrus knocked-up last Thursday from banana leaves stuck together with glue and decorated with Western Christian names or astrological signs as certainly not seen in the tomb of Tutankhamun.

The majority of these shops are to be found in the back streets of the Coptic Christian area of the city and it is here we get back to the subject of Saint George.

When he isn't dragging you into shops, your driver will escort you to what to me is the world's worst tourist attraction, (See Tourist Attractions) a churchyard, known as the City of the Dead, where some half a million poor people live and work amongst the graves. You then get to see the church built over the crypt marking the spot where Mary allegedly lay the Baby Jesus to sleep when they were escaping from the killing of the first-born and then, and then the piece de resistance, a convent boasting the chapel where Saint George was once held captive.

When I visited this chapel I was suffering from a very painful leg complaint, probably due to having to climb from the roads to the pavements in Cairo where they make sure cars don't run into pedestrians by building footpaths at a height requiring crampons and a team of sherpas.

My driver knew about my leg. We had already taken a detour close to the Pyramids where I endured a massage, inhaled exotic fumes from a hubble-bubble pipe and purchased a bottle of a miracle cure that smelt strongly of oil that had recently been used for frying onions. All of this for the equivalent of £40 including the driver's back-hander.

When we arrived at Saint George's chapel a service was in progress. Several hundred worshipers knelt on the stone-flagged floor in front of three nuns who preached to them in Egyptian Arabic.

As soon as they saw the driver and myself standing at the rear of the congregation the service came to an abrupt halt and everyone turned to look as the nuns beckoned the two of us forward to the platform at the front of the church.

They clearly knew the driver and instantly asked him from what illness I was suffering. He pointed at my legs which brought about a mighty shaking of heads and concerned tutting from the nuns. From this reaction the congregation seemed to deduce that I was suffering from some incurable disease and they all started to murmur and make sympathetic noises.

The driver then escorted me to a wall at the side of the altar where he showed me Saint George's chains, a metal collar attached to a heavy chain some four metres in length. He demonstrated George's suffering by placing the collar around his throat and indicating that the poor future saint had to stand in this position for several days, weeks or possibly even months.

He wrapped the chains around my leg with the help of one nun while the other two nuns splashed me with holy water and muttered incantations.

Of course my only wish was to get out of the place so when he asked if my leg felt better I said 'Yes.' This was explained to the congregation who stood and applauded. Some were openly crying, they had just witnessed a miracle. (See Miracles)

The collection plate was produced and it was suggested the equivalent of £10 would be a suitable donation. I dropped two banknotes and a collection of small coins on to the plate, the driver helped himself to his share and we left to continued cheers and tears from the worshipers many of whom tried to touch me as we departed.

I was told by my Cairo guide that Saint George was held prisoner there during the Crusades. The First Crusade began in 1095 AD. Saint George is believed to have died in 281 AD.

Boxer George Foreman has five sons: George Jr, George III, George IV, George V and George VI.

GIMME SHELTER

The council in Exeter, Devon, once revealed that their nuclear fall-out shelter could also be used in case of flooding. They failed to explain whether this shelter was several floors above the ground to keep the water out.

A nuclear fall-out shelter in Kettering, Northamptonshire, had an outside toilet.

GORGEOUS GIRLS

In the 1970s I worked as manager of a nightclub which was selected to host a heat of a beauty competition. Our winner would progress to the nationally televised Miss England event, the winner of this would be the U.K.'s entrant in the international Miss World pageant.

My reward for playing ball in all of this would be to join the eventual potential Miss Worlds for the pre-show dinner and stand by a door as a security guard at the Royal Albert Hall during the final of the competition.

I was given strict instructions from the organisers about the Miss England heat at my club.

Judges were to be a sporting personality, a TV star and myself.

For several weeks prior to the big night I was to be found

chatting to pretty girls in the club encouraging them to enter for this prestigious title. They would be required to appear on stage in a smart cocktail dress or evening gown, then there would be a second appearance in a swimsuit and finally they would be interviewed, still wearing their swimsuit, by our house DJ. He was given a preprepared script probing the contestants' hobbies, favourite pets and what they would do to change the world.

We had eight contestants. Seven girls who regularly came to my club plus an outsider who turned up unannounced on the night.

The eight girls, all of them extremely good looking, were escorted to the room next-door to my office which was to be their changing room. In the interest of fair play I popped in to make sure everything was okay and this is when I noticed that the outsider had with her a hairdresser, make-up artist, plus someone applying a head-to-toe spray tan.

I had been told in advance how I had to vote. It was expected that the captain of Exeter City FC and a TV weather girl would follow the national average at these events and spread most of their votes between five and seven points out of ten in each of the three categories. They would not be cruel enough to give a mark below five and unlikely to favour one girl sufficiently to mark her above eight.

My instruction was that the local girls would end up looking like idiots if they had to appear on national television in front of a theatre audience so I had to save them this humiliation by giving all of them votes of zero and awarding ten points in all three categories to the out of towner.

Obviously statistically she couldn't lose and she didn't.

Miss World is the oldest international beauty pageant. In the days I was involved it was still being run by its creator Eric Morley. When Eric died in 2000 it was taken over by his widow Julia. I am sure the fixing of results is very much a thing of the past.

National and international beauty competitions have been banned as degrading to women in Canada since 1992.

The 1959 Ilfracombe Carnival Bathing Belle Competition was won by 50-year-old grandmother Ethel Vickery. Mrs Vickery said she had no idea why more carnival souvenir brochures containing the Bathing Belle voting slips had been sold than there were people in attendance and she denied any attempt to rig the result.

The sixteen other entrants, average age 18, raised no objections to the result, although one did unsportingly remark that Mrs Vickery's swimming costume contained sufficient material to make costumes for any three of the other girls.

After being booed off stage and threatened she would be pelted with rotten fruit and eggs if she rode through the town on the Carnival Queen float, Mrs Vickery still refused to give up her winner's sash and £10 prize.

The beauty queen float was cancelled but by way of compensation Mrs Vickery was allowed to lead the Ilfracombe Floral Dance which was accompanied by the local brass band who dropped the customary 'Floral Dance' music in favour of 'For She's a Jolly Good Granny.'

GRAFFITI

Graffiti is the plural of graffito.

Graffiti and graffito takes their names from the Italian word 'graffiato,' meaning 'scratched.'

A law in Texas makes it illegal to paint graffiti on someone else's cow.

Graffiti scratched by Lord Byron can still be seen on columns of the Temple of Poseidon in Attica, Greece.

One of the upright stones at Stonehenge has graffiti 'X Wren' said to have been carved by Sir Christopher Wren (X being an abbreviation of Christos or Christopher (See Xmas)) who lived 15 miles away. By coincidence (or is it?) the diameter of the Sarsen Circle at Stonehenge is 102 feet, the same as the inner dome at Wren's St Paul's Cathedral. (See Domes)

Modern-day graffiti artists like to be called writers.

Graffiti is the fourth element of hip hop, along with DJing, emceeing and break dancing.

Graffiti artists making their first marks on walls in an area are known by more experienced writers as 'toys.'

Graffiti with bubble writing as we see it today, sprayed on bridges, walls and trains, began in Philadelphia in the late 1960s.

A graffiti artist's signature is his tag. One of the first well-known graffiti artists was Darryl McCray who went by the tag Cornbread.

Many graffiti artists use large rubber stamps to speed up the process. Others, like Banksy, create their work with stencils. Some believe this defies the true nature of graffiti.

GREAT FIRES

Books and websites accessed for my research variously list the number of deaths in the Great Fire of London as 4, 5, 6, 7, 10, 11 and 12. A telephone call to the British Museum gave their most recent estimate of Great Fire deaths as 9.

Robert Hubert was hanged for starting the Great Fire of London, a crime he was later proved to be innocent of.

In 2004 some 300 people died in a fire at a supermarket in Asuncion, Paraguay. When the fire started the owner shut the doors so customers couldn't get out without paying.

A natural gas vent has been continuously burning in Iraq for more than 4,000 years and is known as the Eternal Fire. It is mentioned in the Book of Daniel in the Old Testament.

Don't try this at home but the movie image of someone generating a huge ball of fire by tossing a cigarette end into a pool of petrol (gasoline) is a fallacy. Researchers made 2,000 attempts to ignite a petrol puddle with a smouldering cigarette butt with no success.

Here's one you can try at home folks. Super glue can set fire to cotton. Hold a cotton bud over a saucer of water (health and safety) and apply drops of super glue.

Burning Mountain is the common name for Mount Wingen in New South Wales, Australia. It takes its name from an underground smouldering coal seam estimated to have been burning for 6,000 years.

This, the oldest known coal fire in the world, travels at about 1 metre per year in a southerly direction.

There is no record of who invented the fire hydrant. Its patent was destroyed in a fire.

HABITS

Charles Darwin cut down on his snuff taking habit by keeping his snuff box in the cellar and its key in the attic.

Scientists say gossiping is a useful habit that brings people closer together. Oxford University primatologist Robin Dunbar claims gossip between humans is the equivalent of primates grooming one another.

Psychologists have discovered that it's an automatic human habit to look up and to the left when you tell a lie.

Although most adult look upon kids playing video games as a bad habit, psychologists say such play increases creativity.

HALLOWE'EN

Pumpkin carving was invented by the Irish. They originally carved swedes (turnips) then when they emigrated to the States they discovered pumpkins were softer and easier to carve.

Americans call a carved pumpkin a Jack-o-lantern. Jack-o-lantern derives from a character in British folklore. This was the soul of someone who was barred from entering both heaven and hell and was condemned to walk the Earth at night carrying his lantern.

99% of all pumpkins sold in the US and Canada are purchased for the purpose of carving for decoration.

Although many British people complain that trick or treat is an American custom imported here, children in the North of England enjoyed Mischief Night in early November. They would play pranks on neighbours while collecting money to spend on fireworks for Guy Fawkes' Night on November 5th.

Mischief Night was practiced long before the birth of Guy Fawkes and long before Europeans reached the USA.

HAEMORRHOIDS

Explorer David Livingstone is the only historically important person to have died from haemorrhoids. This was officially described as 'bleeding due to dysentery.'

Haemorrhoids were responsible for Napoleon's defeat at Waterloo as he was in so much pain he could not view the battlefield from the height of his horse's back

Johnny Cash's estate refused permission for a company to use his song 'Ring of Fire' for a haemorrhoid cream commercial.

HAIR

An acersecomic is someone who has never had their hair cut.

Rapper Tupac Shakur - who was shot dead in 1996 at the age of 25 - adopted his signature shaven head to hide the fact he was going bald. (See Dance)

Every evening the mother of child actress Shirley Temple set her daughter's hair in precisely 56 curls.

Many museums display what they refer to as stone 'pillows' from the ancient Egyptian era. These items did not support the head, they were neck rests designed to avoid disturbance to exotic hairstyles.

HARRY POTTER

Michael Jackson wanted to write 'Harry Potter - the Musical', J.K. Rowling turned him down. Rowling does not refer to Zombies in any Harry Potter book because she associates these too closely with Michael Jackson's 'Thriller'.

Plants referred to in the Wizarding world come from an actual book. 'Culpeper's Complete Herbal', written in the 17th century by English botanist Nicholas Culpeper. Rowling said she collected the names of plants that sounded 'witchy' and in 'Culpeper's' she found such plants as, Toadflax, Gout-wort, Mugwort and Flax weed.

The title 'Harry Potter and the Philosopher's Stone' was changed in the USA because the publishers were concerned American readers would not understand the term 'Philosopher's Stone'. After rejecting a suggestion the book should be retitled 'Harry Potter and the School of Magic', it was decided Americans would go for 'Harry Potter and the Sorcerer's Stone', which is the US book title and the title of the associated movie.

In the books Harry has green eyes, in the movies they are blue.

In French Harry Potter books Voldemort's middle name is Elvis.

J.K. Rowling, when asked by a fan why Hogwarts' headmaster Dumbledore never married, said it was because she always thought of him as gay.

Steven Spielberg was originally slated to direct the Harry Potter films and his chosen actor to play the title role was 'Sixth Sense' star Haley Joel Osment.

J.K. Rowling came up with the names of the Hogwarts houses on an aircraft. She wrote down the names she had devised on the back of a sick bag.

The creepy Dementors who feed on human emotions were inspired by depression Rowling suffered following the death of her mother.

HEADLINE NEWS

When Labour politician Michael Foot was appointed head of a disarmament committee in 1986 The Times ran the headline 'Foot Heads Arms Body.'

'Man With No Arms or Legs is Armed and on the Run' — The Fugitive, Florida.

'Pug Starts Fight With Police Dog After 4-Hour Stand-Off' —

The Real Story

'Bugs Flying Around With Wings Are Flying Bugs' —
Redwood Co. Extension Educator

'Man Threw Snail at Car in Street Row' — Chester Leader

'My Dead Nan Appeared on a Naan' — Metro

'I've Been Posting My Letters in the Dog Poo Bin for Two
Years' — Star

'Florida Woman Calls 911 After McDonald's Runs Out of
McNuggets' — Fox News

'Statistics Show Teen Pregnancy Drops Off Significantly After
Age 25' — Colorado Springs

HENRY VIII

Henry VIII had an annual drinks bill of £6 million in present
day terms and a meat bill of £3.5 million. In later life his
estimated daily intake was 5,000 calories.

Henry VIII was the first British monarch to be born in
a hospital. However, it has to be said that what became
Greenwich Hospital was then Greenwich Palace and is now
the Royal Naval Training College.

Despite a whole host of sources claiming Henry VIII was the

founder of the Royal Navy, he wasn't. The Royal Navy already existed but Henry's investment increased its size ten-fold because he feared attacks from Spain and France following his separation from Rome.

Henry VIII was married to his first wife, Katherine of Aragon, for 22 years which is longer than his later five marriages combined.

HERBS AND SPICES

Nobody can explain why Americans call herbs 'erbs'.

If you are stuffing your Christmas turkey with sage and onion don't chop up your sage until you have gone through the following ceremony. On the dot of midnight Christmas Eve (I am also told this works at noon on 24th April which is St Marks' Eve) pick a sage leaf each time the clock chimes. If you can pick all twelve leaves without damaging any of them an image of your future marriage partner will appear behind you.

Almost all the wasabi served alongside sushi in British and US restaurants and sold in supermarket sushi packs is horseradish dyed green. (See Japan)

The heat of chili peppers is measured on the Scoville Scale. Every year someone seems to come up with a hotter chili so none are listed here as record holders, due to the likelihood of being overtaken. The hottest chilis require careful handling as they can eat their way through latex gloves.

The herb epazote reduces the gassy problems associated with

eating beans. (See Petomane)

Allspice comes from a single berry, it is not a blend of several spices.

Ancient Greeks believed basil would only grow if you shouted curses at it as you sowed the seeds.

It was illegal to import Sichuan peppercorns into the USA until 2005.

Sichuan peppercorns (Known as Szechwan pepper or Chinese pepper in the US) are not peppercorns, they are the outer husks of seeds from the prickly ash shrub.

Turmeric, the spice found in curry that leaves unremovable stains down the front of your shirt if you are a messy eater, has been found to outperform all known drugs in its effectiveness against Alzheimer's symptoms.

Saffron, the most expensive of all spices, is the stamen of an Autumn crocus. One pound, (450g) of dried saffron takes 20 hours of labour and 75,000 flowers.

The second-most expensive spice is vanilla.

It is a particular gene found in some people that makes them have a strong aversion to the herb coriander. Some people love the herb, those with the gene think it smells like soap or cat urine.

A 2016 survey found 64% of those surveyed disliked what they were told to be coriander leaves but only 49% disliked what they were told was cilantro. Coriander and cilantro are the same thing.

Fenugreek promotes lactation in nursing mothers and it makes your urine smell like maple syrup. (See Urine)

HIP-HIP-HOORAY

'Hip-hip-hooray' originated in the battle-cry of the Crusaders. Their shout of 'Hierosolyma est Perdita', meaning 'Jerusalem has fallen' was shortened by Germanic tribes fighting Jews to 'Hep Hep Huraj'.

HITLER

Hitler's documents were typed on a machine with letters three times the usual size.

Hitler's favourite movie was 'King Kong'.

Adolf Hitler was a vegetarian. The Buddha wasn't.

Germany didn't declare Hitler to be officially dead until 1956.

Hitler received a school report describing him as 'bad tempered' and observing, 'he fancies himself as a leader'.

The GoodReads website listed Hitler's 'Mein Kampf' as the second-worst read ever. 'Dianetics' by L. Ron Hubbard topped their list.

A German businessman who trained his dog to give a Hitler salute was given 13 months probation.

Pope Pius XII performed a distant exorcism on Adolf Hitler. It didn't work!

Adolf Hitler had Irish relatives including the son of his brother Alois, known as Paddy Hitler. Paddy's mother, Bridget Hitler, claimed Adolf visited them when they lived in Liverpool and she was responsible for telling the future Fuhrer he should clip his handlebar moustache into the toothbrush shape for which he became famous.

HOGMANAY

This will probably kill any chance of sales of this book in Scotland but Hogmanay originates from an old French New Year gift-giving custom called Hoguinana.

Robert Burns is always credited with writing the song sung around the world at midnight on New Year's Eve. He might well have written the words but the tune of 'Auld Lang Syne' had been around for at least 80 years before Burns published his version in 1788.

To ensure luck in the coming year the first person through your door on January first (known as First Footing) should be male, dark of hair and skin, and should bring a gift of a piece of coal, small silver coin and some salt. He should be rewarded with something sweet to eat and a glass of whisky.

HOMER SIMPSON - THE WIT AND WISDOM

'Homer no function beer well without.'

'Every time I learn something new it pushes some old stuff out of my brain. Remember when I took that home winemaking course and I forgot how to drive?'

'Oh boy dinnertime. The perfect break between work and drunk.'

'Maybe, just once, someone will call me 'Sir' without adding,' You're making a scene'.

'Im not a bad guy. I work hard and I love my kids. So why should I spend half my Sunday hearing about how I'm going to Hell?'

'Oh, so they have internet on computers now.'

'To start press any key. Where's the 'ANY' key?'

'Marge, don't discourage the boy. Weaselling out of things is important to learn. It's what separates us from animals. Except the weasel.'

'Son, if you really want something in this life you have to work for it. Now be quiet they're about to announce the lottery numbers.'

'Son, when you participate in sporting events it's not whether you win or lose: it's how drunk you get.'

'I'm trying to be a sensitive father you unwanted moron.'

'I'm not normally a praying man but if you're up there please save me, Superman.'

'Just because I don't care doesn't mean I don't understand.'

'It's one a.m. Better go home and spend some quality time with the kids.'

'Old people don't need companionship. They need to be isolated and studied so it can be determined what nutrients they have that might be extracted for our personal use.'

'Lisa, if you don't like your job you don't strike. You go in every day and do it really half-assed. That's the American way.'

'Lisa, if the Bible has taught us anything, and it hasn't, it's that girls should stick to girls' sports such as hot oil wrestling and foxy boxing.'

'Lisa, vampires are make-believe like elves, gremlins and eskimos.'

(On meeting aliens) 'Please don't eat me I have a wife and kids. Eat them.'

'The three little sentences that will get you through life. Number 1: 'Cover for me.' Number 2: 'Oh good idea boss.' Number 3: 'It was like that when I got here.'

In France Homer's 'D'oh!' is dubbed as 'T'oh!'.

(See Simpson Quotes)

HONEYMOONERS

Honeymoons take their name from an old German custom that involved drinking vast quantities of the honey-based drink mead following one's wedding?

Attila the Hun is reputed to have died of alcohol poisoning during his thirty-day honeymoon binge.

Ethelred the Unready was clearly more ready than history gives him credit for. On his wedding night he was found in bed with his new wife and her mother.

HORSE RACING

The name of a racehorse cannot contain more than 18 letters and spaces.

British bookmakers estimate £500,000 of winning bets are not claimed annually due to punters losing their tickets or not even realising they have won.

The Grand National has been won more times by horses with names starting with R than any other.

HOT, HOT, HOT

The Northern Hemisphere is 1.5C warmer than the Southern Hemisphere.

Some cacti have the ability to move underground if things get too hot.

HUMAN BODY

The navel of the average human baby is half way between the top of the head and the tip of the toes.

Although sunburn appears to heal after a couple of days it takes 15 months for the blood vessels beneath the skin to return to normal.

A foetus in the womb can hiccup.

Reading about yawning can make you yawn.

Every day we forget 80% of what we have learned. (See Homer Simpson - The Wit and Wisdom)

Hold your breath and lower your face into a bowl of cold water. Your heart immediately slows down by 25%.

You replace each of your taste buds every ten days.

The bacteria in your ears increases 700-fold after wearing headphones for one hour.

When you are frightened by something your ears secrete more wax.

Most Koreans lack the gene that produces stinky armpits.

Your wanus is your little finger.

HUMP

Abdul Kassel Ismael, Grand Vizier of Persia in the latter half of the tenth century, had a 117,000-book library that followed him throughout his kingdom. The books were carried on 400 camels trained to walk in alphabetical order.

Camels are multi-purpose beasts. You can drink their milk, make leather with their hide, make clothes with their hair and their dung makes a very good fire.

A camel's hump is filled with fat, not water.

Camels have a multi-chambered stomach like cows. They need to regurgitate and chew the cud, which is why they are led by a rope or halter at the nose rather than in the mouth, in order not to interfere when they chew.

Camels can close their nostrils to keep out sand. They have two sets of lashes to protect their eyes.

I

IMMIGRATION

The first immigrants from Asia crossed the Bering Straits in around 15,000BC.

Britain has only been an island for approximately 7,000 years making it possible for anyone to come and go freely and making all of the current population the ancestors of immigrants.

IMMORTALITY

'I do not want to achieve immortality through my work. I want to achieve immortality by not dying.' — Woody Allen

In the 3rd century BC Chinese Emperor Qin Shi Huang, of Terracotta Army fame, took regular doses of mercury believing it would give him eternal life. It didn't.

INFLATION

The entrance fee to Kew Gardens was one penny until 1980 when it was increased to ten pence. At the time of writing in 2017 the price for an adult ticket at the gate is £16.50 including a £1.50 voluntary donation.

INSECTS

Termites are attracted to the smell of the ink in ballpoints pens.

If all the termites in the world were gathered together and weighed their total weight would equal ten times that of all the humans.

Termite farts are one of the main contributors to holes in the ozone layer. (See Petomane)

There are more than 380,000 species of beetles.

Beetles have no taste buds.

Male fruit flies enjoy a drop of alcohol but it turns them homosexual.

Insects don't breathe through noses. They have holes called spiracles, usually in lines along their abdomen and thorax.

Crickets and grasshoppers have ears on their legs.

Honeybees have hairy eyes.

A nighttime butterfly has ears on its wings to help it steer clear of bats.

A locust can eat its own bodyweight of food in a day. A human takes six months to eat his/her bodyweight.

East African Vampire Spiders get the blood they require by eating mosquitoes that have sucked blood from a person or animal.

A hercules beetle can lift 850 times its own weight. This is equivalent to a human lifting ten adult elephants.

There are 1.4 million ants to every human on the planet.

A wingless midge called Belgica Antarctica is the only true insect species to call the Antarctic its home.

Midges are tiny blood-sucking flies. Midges can beat their wings faster than any other creature, one type beats its wings 1,000 times per second.

INSULTS

'A shiver looking for a spine to run up.' — Harold Wilson on Edward Heath

'He sings like he's throwing up.' — Comedian/actor Andrew O'Connor on Bryan Ferry

'A semi-house-trained polecat.' — Michael Foot on Norman Tebbit

'If I found her floating in my pool I'd punish the dog.' — Joan Rivers on Yoko Ono

'I've met serial killers and assassins but nobody scared me as much as Mrs Thatcher.' — Ken Livingstone

'More a ventriloquist's dummy than a Prime Minister.' — Tory

MP Sir Nicholas Fairbairn's description of Tory MP John Major.

'I'm reserving two tickets for you for my premiers. Come and bring a friend - if you have one.' — George Bernard Shaw to Winston Churchill.

'Impossible to be present for the first performance. Will attend the second - if there is one.' — Churchill's reply to the above.

'The album was only called 'Bad' because there wasn't enough space on the sleeve for 'Pathetic'.' — Prince on Michael Jackson

'People ask me, 'Is Boris a very, very clever man pretending to be an idiot? I always answer, 'No'.' — Ian Hislop on Boris Johnson

'A pound shop Enoch Powell.' — Russell Brand on Nigel Farage

'Do you mind if I sit back a little because your breath is very bad.' — Donald Trump to US TV interviewer Larry King

INVENTIONS

The screwdriver was invented before the screw.

The Super Soaker water pistol was invented out of PVC piping and Coke bottles by nuclear engineer Lonnie Johnson.

Play-Doh originated as a wallpaper cleaner.

1930s/40s movie glamour star Hedy Lamarr, helped develop frequency-hopping technology which is crucial to such modern essentials as mobile phones and GPS devices.

Scientist and politician Isaac Newton invented the cat flap.

William Morrison invented the machine that turns sugar into candy floss (cotton candy). Morrison was a dentist!

The inflatable doll was invented to counterbalance the sexual desires of Nazi troops. The original dolls were named Borghild and had white skin, blue eyes and blonde hair to reflect the Nazi's ideal beauty.

Bubble Wrap came as a result of Alfred Fielding and Marc Chavannes' unsuccessful attempt to produce 3D plastic wallpaper.

Most bubble gum is pink because this was the only food colouring its inventor Walter E. Diemer had to hand and it's stuck.

Liquid Paper correction fluid was invented by the mother of Mike Nesmith from the Monkees pop group.

Thomas Jefferson invented the swivel chair.

J

JAPAN

Japan consists of more than 6,800 islands and has more than 3,000 McDonald's restaurants.

KFC has been an accepted Christmas dish in Japan since people confused Colonel Sanders with Santa Claus.

Morning commuters in Japan are often handed tissues printed with advertisements. The tissues are welcomed because public toilets usually have no hand tissues or toilet paper.

Japan uses more paper for comic books than for toilet paper.

There are 50,000+ people in Japan over the age of 100.

The UK has eight annual Bank Holidays, Japan has 16. Japanese Bank Holidays include; Coming-of-Age-Day, Vernal Equinox Day, Respect for the Aged Day and The Emperor's Birthday.

Japanese will tell you that their dogs go 'wan-wan' not 'bow-wow'.

90% of mobile phones sold in Japan are waterproofed so they can be used in the shower.

It is acceptable to fall asleep at work in Japan. It is viewed as a sign of exhaustion from working hard.

Crooked teeth, known as Yaeba, are so popular in Japan that many girls go to cosmetic dentists who specialise in unstraightening teeth. At one time Japanese women blackened their teeth as a fashion statement.

Frogs are a symbol of good luck in Japan.

The Japanese look upon their belly as the centre of emotions rather than the heart.

Sushi does not mean raw fish, it means seasoned rice. Raw fish is sashimi.

Wasabi was only originally served with sashimi and sushi to kill parasites in the fish. (See Herbs and Spices)

Traditionally Japanese restaurants do not employ female sushi chefs because women's hands are allegedly too warm to roll the rice..

Tempura was introduced to Japan by Portuguese missionaries in the 16th century.

Be prepared if you're ever invited to attend a Japanese

Nantaimori banquet. Guests help themselves to a buffet of sushi and sashimi tastefully displayed on the naked body of a beautiful girl.

Hello Kitty, known locally as 'Kitty Chan', was first introduced in Japan in 1974. The first Hello Kitty product was a plastic purse.

Japan has more pensioners (over 65) than children. The people buy more nappies for adults than for babies.

Tokyo's Shinjuku railway station is the busiest in the world with as many as two million passengers in a single day.

'Mayo No I-rando', 'Magic Island', by Yume-Hotaru, published in 1993, was the first novel written entirely on a mobile phone.

JAWS

The original title of Peter Benchley's book 'Jaws' was 'Silence of the Deep.'

When Steven Spielberg first saw the book he thought 'Jaws' was going to be a horror story about a dentist.

'Jaws' is described by some as Steven Spielberg's greatest movie masterpiece. It is essential to the plot that the action takes place in the build-up to the celebrations of Independence Day, the Fourth of July. Realising that holiday crowds would interfere with filming, 27-year-old Spielberg made 'Jaws' in the middle of winter.

The above explains why Amity Island, filmed at a coastal town near Martha's Vineyard, just to the south of Cape Cod, celebrates Independence Day against a background of leafless trees.

The not very good model of a shark, called Bruce by the crew, was used instead of a real shark because at the time the longest a real white shark had been kept in captivity before dying was eleven days.

The first model shark sank and was given the nicknamed 'Flaws' or the 'Great White Turd,' by the crew.

JOINTS

Everyone knows someone who claims to be double-jointed but there is no such thing. Some people do have more elasticity in the tissues connecting their bones but there is no medical record to support actual double joints.

KISMET

Nelson died in the arms of his flag-captain Thomas Masterson Hardy shortly after being told that victory was certain. What he actually said was 'Kismet (i.e. destiny) Hardy,' not 'Kiss me Hardy.'

The 1953 musical 'Kismet' has tunes adapted from the music of Borodin. Although regularly resurrected by am-dram societies the only song most people can remember is 'Stranger in Paradise,' or 'Strange Looking Parasite' as Spike Milligan would have it. (See Award Ceremonies)

KUBLA KHAN

Samuel Taylor Coleridge rented a cottage at Lynton, North Devon, to convalesce following some unspecified illness. The great poet treated even minor maladies with opium and one afternoon, whilst in a drug-induced sleep, he saw all 300 lines of 'The Greatest Work of English Literature' written out before him in his dream.

Recovering from his nap Coleridge put pen to paper to record the epic work for posterity.

As every literary scholar is aware, it was at this point Coleridge was interrupted by 'A Man From Porlock' who spent an hour trying to sell him insurance.

This is why 'Kubla Khan', 'The Greatest Work of English Literature,' disappeared from the poet's memory and peters out after 54 lines.

L

L.A.

'El Pueblo de Nuestra Señora la Reina de los Angeles la Porciuncula' is the full name of the city universally known as L.A. The name means 'The town of Our Lady the Queen of the Angels of the Little Portion.' 'Little Portion' is alternatively translated as 'Porciuncula River.'

Oil was discovered in 1892 close to where the Dodgers Stadium now stands. In 1923 L.A. was producing a quarter of the world's oil and still stands on the USA's third-largest oil deposit.

The L.A. Coroner's Office has a gift shop.

It is illegal to lick a toad in L.A. (See LAW)

The famous HOLLYWOOD sign originally read HOLLYWOODLAND and was an advertisement for a real estate development.

The HOLLYWOOD sign was designed by an English landscape artist, Thomas Fisk Goff

In 1978 the HOLLYWOOD sign required a major overhaul, money wasn't available and it looked as though the sign would have to be pulled down. Playboy boss Hugh Hefner held a fundraiser at which businessmen and celebrities paid $28,000 each to adopt a letter. Among the famous who supported letters are: O - Alice Cooper, L - Gene Autrey, Y - Hugh Hefner, W - Andy Williams. The sign is now supported by its own trust fund.

The Getty Museum in L.A. employs goats every spring to cut the grass.

LAKES

Limnology is the study of lakes and other freshwater features.

Lake Baikal in Russia contains sufficient water to supply the entire world's needs for fifty years.

Isle Royale in the centre of Lake Superior has its own lakes.

Lake Michigan is the only Great Lake entirely in America.

The Canadian province Ontario was named after the lake and not the other way around.

In autumn the upper layer of lakes cool down due to winds. The warmer layer at the bottom then rises to the surface mixing cold and warm on its way. This process is known as turnover.

LAND'S END TO JOHN O'GROATS

Sportsmen and charity fund raisers regularly make the trip

from Land's End to John O'Groats, or visa versa, believing these to be the most southerly and northerly points in Britain. They're not. Britain's most southerly spot is Lizard Point and the most northerly is Duncansby Head.

There is a dispute between sources, Google Maps and several others say the quickest road distance from Land's End to John O'Groats is 837 miles (1,349km). The famous sign posts at both ends of the journey give the distance as 874 mile (1,407 km).

Both of the above distances involve sections of motorway so cyclists and walkers could not use these routes.

As the crow flies the distance between Land's End and John O'Groats is 603 miles

The official name of Land's End is Peal Point. It is known locally as The Peal.

In 2012 Land's End was the starting point for the Olympic torch relay.

Most visitors to Land's End head for the hotel and tourist complex. These are at Carn Kez, approximately 200 metres south of Land's End.

Cape Cornwall to the north of Land's End is England's only cape.

John O'Groats takes its name from a 16th century Dutch immigrant called Jan de Groot. John (to give him his British name) had seven offspring who constantly argued over their precedence. John solved the problem by building an octagonal house with eight doors so he and his family could each leave or enter at the same time. He solved the problem of who sat at the head of the table by constructing an octagonal piece of furniture from which to dine. This unusual house sat on a mound close to what is now the John O'Groats House Hotel.

People who live at John O'Groats are known as Groaters.

LANGUAGE

There are around 7,000 different languages in the world.

Approximately 12.5% of the world's population speak Mandarin as their first language.

The Vatican city has ATMs with a Latin option.

Botswana has a language consisting of five different clicks.

American sign language has separate version for black people and white people.

Bookkeeper and bookkeeping are the only words in the English language with three consecutive double letters.

The E.U. has 234 working languages.

The French have 13 different ways of pronouncing the letter 'o' when it appears in a word.

Twirk (not twerk) is a 16th century word for playing with the ends of your moustache.

The dot over the letter 'i' is a tittle.

LAW

In Alabama it is illegal to wear a false moustache that causes people to laugh in church.

Several US states have laws making it illegal to dance to 'The Star Spangled Banner.'

The minimum age of marriage for girls in Italy was raised to twelve in 1892. (See Child Brides)

Scandinavian law prevents advertisements selling food to children.

Singapore has cleaned up air pollution by increasing tax on cars as they get older and by banning all cars over the age of eight years.

In Indiana it is illegal for a bar to serve drinks on the house.

Sticking chewing gum under a seat on the upper deck of a London bus can be punished by 24-hours imprisonment.

In Somalia it is illegal to stick chewed gum on the end of your nose.

Only dental or nicotine chewing gum are legal in Singapore.

It is illegal for anyone to enter the state of Wisconsin with a chicken on their head.

The USA is so pro military veterans that in 2010 a man in Pennsylvania was charged with breaking a trooper's fist with his face.

In Montana you are not allowed to have a sheep in the cab of your truck unless a chaperone is travelling with you.

In New Hampshire it is not permitted to trade the clothes you are wearing to pay off a gambling debt.

In New York you require a licence to hang out clothes on a clothes line.

Maine has a law making it illegal to step out of a plane in flight.

In Minnesota bathtubs must stand on feet. (See Bathrooms)

LETTERS

In 1976 Idi Amin wrote a letter to Lord Snowdon which included the sentiment: 'Your experience will be a lesson to us all not to marry ladies of high position.' (See Margarets)

During the sixteen years it took Snowdon to break up with Princess Margaret he used to write letters and leave them between the pages of books for his wife to find. These were invariably based on the theme, 'Things I hate about you.'

LITTLE BASTARD

James Dean died in 1955 when his Porsche 550 Spyder, named 'Little Bastard', was involved in a head-on collision with another vehicle.

After the accident the Porsche was purchased by a garage owner, George Barris, whose mechanic's leg was broken when the car slipped as it was being unloaded from a breakdown truck.

Barris sold the engine to a doctor who was killed when the vehicle he installed it in ran out of control during a race. This same race included a car into which Dean's drive-shaft had been fitted, that car also crashed and the driver was seriously injured.

The body of Dean's Porsche was taken around the country as part of a road safety exhibition. It fell off a stand in Sacramento breaking a young man's hip. During the same safety tour the car body rolled off a truck that was carrying it, killing the driver.

The racing driver who bought the Porsche tyres was almost killed when two of them burst simultaneously.

The remains of the car finally vanished completely whilst being carried to Los Angeles by train.

Claims that Little Bastard had been discovered in 2015 are disputed at the time of writing.

LITTLE LAMB

There was a fad for injecting foetal cells from a lamb to prevent ageing. Winston Churchill, Charlie Chaplin and Christian Dior underwent this treatment. It didn't work.

In 2007 the average American ate 86.5 pounds of chicken, 65 pounds of beef, 50.5 pounds of pork, 17.3 pounds of turkey but only 1.1 pounds of lamb.

Sheep can recognise human faces.

Raising sheep is the oldest organised industry.

Wool has been used for human clothing for more than 10,000 years. When the Romans first visited Britain in 55BC British people were already famous for the softness of their clothes made from wool.

Sheep can see behind themselves without turning their heads.

Christopher Columbus came from a family of wool traders and it was the wool industry that funded his expeditions to the New World. Columbus took the first sheep to the US in 1493.

The life expectancy of sheep is from six to eleven years.

LOVE, LOVE, LOVE

If you fall for someone without a common language it might just help if you can make a start at communicating by saying 'I love you.' The following list should be useful if you get around quite a bit.

Afrikaans — Ek het jou lief

Albanian — Te dua

Arabic to a man — Ana behibak

Arabic to a woman — Ana behibek

Bangla — Aamee tuma ke bhalo basshi

Bulgarian — Obicham te

Cambodian   to a man — Oun Srorlagn Bung

Cambodian to a woman — Bung Storlagn Oun

Cantonese — Ngo oil new a

Catalan — T'estimo

Creole — Mi aime jou

Croatian — Volim te

Czech   — Miluji te

Danish — Jeg Elsker Dig

Dutch   — Ik hou van jou

Esperanto — Mi amas vin

Ethiopian to a man — Ewedihalehu

Ethiopian to a woman — Ewedishalehu

Farsi — Doset daram

Filipino — Mahal kita

Finnish — Mina rakastan sinua

French — Je t'aime

Gaelic — Ta pra agam ort

German — Ich liebe dich

Greek — S'agape

Hawaiian — Aloha was is oi

Hebrew to man — Ani ohev et otcha

Hebrew to woman — Ani ohev otach

Hindi — Hum Tumhe Pyar Karte hai

Hungarian — Szeretlek

Icelandic — Eg elska tig

Indonesian — Saya cinta padamu

Irish — Taim i' agra leat

Italian — Ti amo

Japanese — Aishiteru

Korean — Sarang Heyo

Latvian — Es nevi miilu

Lebanese — Bahibak

Lithuanian — Tave milieu

Malay — Saya cintakan mu

Mandarin — Wo ai ni

Moroccan — Ana moajaba bis

Nepali — Ma Timilai Maya Garchhu

Norwegian — Jeg Elsker Deg

Polish — Kocham Cie

Portuguese — Eu te amo

Romanian — Te iubsec

Russian — Ya tebya liubliu

Scot Gaelic — Tha gradh agam ort

Serbian — Volim te

Slovak — Lu 'bim ta

Slovenian — Ljubim te

Spanish — Te quiero / Te amo

Surinam — Mi lobi joe

Swahili — Ninapenda wewe

Swedish — Jag alskar dig

Swiss-German — Ich leib Di

Tahitian — Ua here vau la oe

Taiwanese — Wa ga ei li

Tamil — Naan annual kathalikiraen

Thai to man — Chan rak khun

Thai to woman — Phom ran shun

Turkish — Seni Seviyorum

Ukrainian — Ya tube kahayu

Vietnamese to man — Em ye u anh

Vietnamese to woman — Anh ye u em

Welsh — 'Rwy'n dy garu

Yiddish — Ike hob dikh

Zimbabwe — Ndinokuda

In Peru, frog juice, made by putting frogs in a blender, is considered to be an aphrodisiac.

LOVE TOKENS

If you carve your initials plus those of your loved one in the bark of the trunk of a tree they will stay at approximately the same height from the ground, no matter how many years later you go back to take a look or make a change.

In Venezuela love letters can be posted for half price if in a pink envelope.

M

MAD AS A HATTER

Lewis Carroll's 'Alice's Adventures in Wonderland' includes a character The Mad Hatter. 'Mad as a hatter' was a common phrase many years prior to the novel.

In the 18th and 19th centuries hat makers used mercury to stabilise woollen felt. Long term contact with mercury fumes causes a type of poisoning known as Korsakoff's syndrome, also known to have been caused by heavy consumption of alcohol.

Symptoms include, severe memory loss, invented memories, minimal content in conversation and general apathy.

MAD KING

'The Madness of King George' was a hugely successful movie. It didn't hold back when it came to the mental state of the 18th/19th century ruler but it did miss out on a few interesting facts about his relatives.

It is well documented that George III's brother, the Duke of Cumberland, married Olive Wilmot, a clergyman's daughter, then, less than a year later, bigamously married Anne Horton, a widow.

The King had another brother, the Duke of Gloucester, who secretly married the Dowager Countess Waldegrave who was the illegitimate daughter of Prime Minister Robert Walpole's son.

The King's sister, Caroline Matilda, married Christian VII of Denmark and then embarked on an outrageous affair with one of her husband's advisers. She was banished from Denmark and her lover was executed.

Recognising the problems within his own family George III introduced the Royal Marriage Act requiring any member of the Royal Family to seek permission from the sovereign before they can marry.

The planned title of the movie 'The Madness of King George III' was changed to 'The Madness of King George' because it was thought American movie-goers would think it was a sequel and not attend because they'd missed 'The Madness of King George I' and 'The Madness of King George II'.

MAIL

Representatives of the Slovenian and Slovakian embassies in Washington DC have a monthly meeting to exchange wrongly delivered mail.

Thanks to being the first with postage stamps, Britain is the only nation that does not have to print the name of the country on its stamps.

More than 1,000 letters addressed to 'God' arrive at the Israel postal service every year. These are opened and placed in the cracks of the Western (Wailing) Wall. (See Barriers)

Santa Claus replies to letters sent to him at the North Pole. His postal code is HOH OHO.

In 1989 a computer error resulted in 41,000 Parisians receiving letters charging them with extortion, murder and prostitution rather than minor traffic offences.

In 2006, convicted murderer Richard Lee McNair secured himself a job stitching mail bags in a Louisiana prison. He took the opportunity to climb into a crate and successfully mailed himself out of gaol. This was his third gaol break. He had previously escaped by using lip balm as a lubricant to slide off a pair of handcuffs and, on another occasion, had crawled out through a ventilation duct.

Until 1915 it was legal to mail a baby in the US. To save money on a train fare, in 1914 the parents of May Piertorff paid 53 cents to mail the five-year-old child to her grandparents for a visit. She travelled in the train's mail car and was delivered to her grandparents' house.

Sean Bean claims he regularly receives fan letters intended for Rowan Atkinson who is better known as Mr Bean.

MAN WHO BROKE THE BANK

Englishman Charles DeVille Wells is celebrated in the song, 'The Man Who Broke the Bank in Monte Carlo'.

Breaking the Bank involved winning all the funds available at a roulette table. When this happened a black cloth was spread across the table and gambling was stopped until further funds had been brought up from the vaults.

Wells' system was to continue betting on one of the two colours, doubling his stake for every losing spin of the wheel. On the day of his famous bank breaking win his opening stake was £400 and he walked out of the casino with £40,000, worth more than £6 million in present day terms.

Wells was a known fraudster and there is speculation as to whether his mega Monte Carlo jackpot was due to luck or, more likely, he had found a way of cheating.

Wells claimed his system was foolproof but the stakes required for a long losing run are massive.

MARCO POLO

Marco Polo, the explorer, wasn't the first westerner to visit China. Two other Polos, Niccolo Polo and Maffeo Polo had already been there and had met Kublai Khan.

Marco Polo began his travels at the age of seventeen and covered 15,000 miles in 24 years.

Marco Polo had a breed of sheep named after him. (See Little Lamb)

Marco Polo introduced paper money to Europe.

Marco Polo was the name of the Scottish light heavyweight boxing title holder in the early 1980s.

MARGARETS

Margaret Mitchell's original title for 'Gone With the Wind' was 'Baa! Baa! Black Sheep.'

When Queen Elizabeth's younger sister, Princess Margaret, married Antony Armstrong Jones the massive crowd resulted in the wedding parade being slowed to walking pace. When they arrived back at Buckingham Palace it was noticed that someone had scratched a heart into the gleaming, maroon paintwork of the royal Rolls-Royce. (See Letters) (See Margarets)

Princess Margaret requested a low-cost, no-fuss funeral with her body to be cremated at Slough Crematorium in the presence of zero mourners.

Her coffin sat in the Queen's Chapel at Windsor Castle for two days so that friends and family could pay their respects. She was then relocated to the nearby St George's Chapel overnight.

The Dean of Windsor conducted a funeral service at the Castle attended by countless Royals.

Margaret's body was then taken to Slough Crematorium, freshly re-painted for the occasion. Her ashes were placed in a casket that now rests in the tomb of her father, George VI, and her mother, Queen Elizabeth the Queen Mother who died a few weeks after Margaret.

Hardly what she'd requested but at least she got Slough Crematorium redecorated.

MASS HYSTERIA

Scary clown sightings began in the USA and Canada in 2016 and quickly spread across the world via the internet. Many people have a fear of clowns so it wasn't difficult to exploit this fear by reporting that clowns wearing 'evil costumes' were roaming the streets of the world.

A few people saw the humorous side of all this by renting clown costumes and wandering the streets at night. Others didn't see the joke. It is, however, now very obvious that the Clown Scare was a recent example of Mass Hysteria.

During the Middle Ages a French nun started to meow like a cat. Eventually all the other nuns in her convent started to join in for part of every day. Local residents complained but the nuns continued their cacophony until the police threatened to whip them.

When a German nun started biting her companions in the 15th century it wasn't long before the habit (pun intended) spread as far as Holland and Italy.

In 1859 panic spread across the US over young people playing too much chess.

Nuns seem to crop up regularly in cases of mass hysteria. In 1749 there was an outbreak of squirming, screaming and trances at a nunnery in Wurzburg, Germany. This came to an end when a nun was executed for witchcraft.

Sixty students at an 1894 ladies' seminary in Montreal suffered from fits and seizures. Some of these symptoms lasted as long as two months.

People died of heart attacks and exhaustion after dancing nonstop for days without rest during the 1518 Dancing Plague in Strasbourg. (See Dance)

When I was a child my mother used to tell me stories about the Halifax Slasher (I suppose less scary than some of the stuff kids now watch on TV!) In November 1938, not long before I was born, two women in my home town of Halifax, Yorkshire, reported they had been attacked by a man with a mallet . Both said he had bright, shiny buckles on his shoes.

The scare escalated with reports from men and women claiming to have been attacked by a man wielding either a knife or a razor. Many of these victims had cuts to their arms and bodies. The situation was so bad Scotland Yard was called in.

On November 29th one alleged victim admitted to having inflicted injuries upon himself to gain attention. Others then came forward with similar admissions and it became obvious none of the attacks had been real.

Five people were charged with public mischief offences, four were sent to prison.

At a mission-run boarding school in Tanganyika three girls started laughing uncontrollably on 30th January, 1962. Within a few days 95 of the school's 159 pupils, aged between 12 and 18, had been affected by the laugh epidemic. None of the staff suffered but things got so bad the school was closed down on 18th March and pupils were sent home.

The laughing attack now spread to other villages, including one where 217 young people could not control their mirth. The school reopened in May but had to be closed again in June due to further laughing outbreaks.

By July laughing attacks were reported from all over the region including 48 girls at a middle-school and at two nearby boys' schools.

In 2001 thousands of people in New Delhi reported seeing a Monkey Man Monster.

MEASUREMENTS

The Big Mac Index was devised by 'Economist' editor Pam Woodall as a measure of whether a currency was under or overvalued. The Big Mac was used for financial comparisons because it was available in 120 countries.

A hairsbreadth is officially 1/48 inch or 0.05 cm.

The smallest amount of time measurable was known as an atomos which is Greek for 'the twinkling of an eye'.

'The twinkling of an eye,' occurs in the Bible (1 Corinthians 15.52) and in Shakespeare's 'The Merchant of Venice.'

BB, as in BB gun, stands for the size of the pellet. 0.18 inch or 4.57 mm is between B and BBB sizes.

A standard Ten Gallon Hat holds less than one gallon of liquid.

A light year is a measurement of distance, not time. One light year is defined as the distance light travels in a vacuum in one Julian Year.

A Julian Year equals 365.25 days.

The size of diamonds is measured in carats. The word carat is derived from the Greek word keration meaning a carob bean which was a standard weight in ancient Greece. The modern definition of a carat is 200 milligrams. Only one polished diamond in a thousand weighs as much as one carat or more.

Biblical distances are usually measured in cubits. A cubit is the distance between the tip of a man's middle finger and his elbow. This is about 18 inches or 45 centimetres. The cubit is divided into six palms or 24 digits.

Mathematicians jokingly proposed a standard unit for measuring beauty: the millihelen. Inspired by Helen of Troy, a millihelen is defined as 'the amount of beauty required to launch one ship.

Physicist Ted Maiman made the first working laser. He graded the output power of a laser according to how many Gillette razor blades it could burn a hole through. The Gillette is now recognised as the measure of the strength of lasers.

A hobo is a measure of smell. A strong fart is rated at 13 hobos, anything with a strength of 50 or more hobos will cause the person doing the smelling to vomit.

Although most people think of a day as being 24 hours the actual length of a day is 23 hours, 56 minutes, 4.1 seconds.

One Mickey, named after Mickey Mouse, is the length of the smallest detectable movement of a computer mouse, about 1/200 inch or 0.1 mm.

MegaFonzie is a measure of coolness. A MegaFonzie is defined as 1,000 times the coolness of Fonzie on the TV show 'Happy Days'.

A moment was a Medieval measure of time equal to 1.5 minutes.

Proof, as seen on a bottle of booze, originates from the 18th century when distillers proved their drinks were not watered down by using a gunpowder proof. A measure of the alcohol was mixed with an equal quantity of gunpowder and this was then ignited. If the mixture burned it was 'proof' that the alcohol was not diluted.

Today proof in the USA is defined as containing 50% of alcohol by volume. 100-proof Scotch contains 50% alcohol. Although the term 'proof' originated in the UK, the UK now uses the ABV (alcohol by volume) system.

A smidgen is half a pinch or 1/32 of a teaspoon.

MEN ON MOON

There are lots of photos of Buzz Aldrin on the Moon taken by Neil Armstrong but Aldrin took very few of Armstrong as he was sulking at not being the first man on the Moon.

Neil Armstrong's first words when he stepped on to the surface of the Moon were: 'One small step for man, a giant leap for mankind.'

Few people ever question the fact that this statement is totally meaningless.

Armstrong had been given his script to learn but, understandably, in the excitement of the moment, he slipped up and left out one essential letter.

What he should have said was: 'One small step for A man, a giant leap for mankind.'

Due to the exorbitant cost involved, the three Apollo Eleven astronauts had no insurance policies to cover them if things went wrong. In case of an accident the trio signed hundreds of autographs and left these with a trusted friend to sell and provide funds for their families.

President Richard Nixon commissioned a speech, written by William Safire, so he had the appropriate words to inform the US population if the first Moon landing ended in tragedy.

Obviously the lunar landers could not smell anything, other than their personal body odours, when in their spacesuits but they reported that once back in the Lunar Module the dust clinging to their clothing and brought inside on their boots had a very pungent smell. Neil Armstrong described the smell as like that of wet ashes, others said it was more like gunpowder.

It was once claimed a very powerful telescope could see the American flag and other items left on the Moon by Armstrong and Aldrin. Armstrong said he looked out of the window as Aldrin launched the Lunar Module for its journey back to join up with Collins in the Command Module. He said the flag and everything else at the landing site was blasted away by the force from the engines.

US astronauts had orders not to make any Christian references for fear of causing offence to people of other religions viewing the events on TV . Buzz Aldrin was a committed Christian and felt the occasion was too good to miss. As he and Armstrong sat on the Moon awaiting instructions to open the door and take their first small steps, Aldrin produced a miniature flask of wine and a piece of bread. He consumed these while reading from the Gospel of John. This is the first and only celebration of Communion on the Moon.

Astronauts had instructions not to fully close the door of the Lunar Module when stepping on to the Moon. To keep within the crucial weight limit the items on the module were kept to a minimum so there was no external door handle to get back in if the door shut completely.

When they returned to the Lunar Module, Armstrong and Aldrin discovered that a switch on the crucial circuit breaker had snapped off leaving them with no way of igniting the engine. They slept while scientists at NASA tried to think of a way to repair it. When no instant fix idea was available Aldrin jammed his pen into the mechanism and this fired the engine to lift the first men off the Moon.

Eleven of the twelve men who walked on the Moon had been Boy Scouts.

MICKEY MOUSE

Mickey Mouse's original voice was provided by Walt Disney. Disney is widely credited as the sole creator of Mickey but this accolade should be shared with animator Ub Iwerks.

One of the most regularly asked question in TV and pub quizzes is: 'What was the first Mickey Mouse movie.' and the most regularly given and accepted answer is 'Steamboat Willie.'

Mickey and Minnie's first public screen appearances came on May 15th, 1928 in a short titled 'Plane Crazy.' 'Steamboat Willie', the first Disney animated cartoon with synchronised sound, wasn't released until November of that same year.

Mickey Mouse in 'Backnumbers' was the final thing to be seen on British television screens before the service closed down for World War II. There was no announcement, screens simply went blank after Mickey had impersonated Greta Garbo, saying: 'Ah think ah go home.'

MILK

When hand-milking cows it takes an average 345 squirts to produce a gallon of milk.

Despite all of the faddy milks now stocked by supermarkets, 90% of the world's milk still comes from cows.

In 2015 a judge in California denied an injunction filed by customers who discovered that almond milk contained only 2% of material actually from almonds.

Nero's second wife, Pappaea, maintained a herd of 500 asses to provide milk for her to bathe in.

Louis Pasteur developed pasteurisation for beer twenty years before he did the same for milk.

Swedish scientists announced in 1984 that milk yield was noticeably increased when cows were fitted with insecticide discs to discourage flies from buzzing around their heads.

Farmers report that if they give a cow a name it produces 450 pints more milk per year than those that remain nameless.

MIRACLE

Calatina del Toro Lopez of Mula in Spain, turned her home into a place of pilgrimage when she regained her voice after being completely dumb for over seven years. Calatina said it was the will of God that she should speak again as her voice had returned when a picture of the Virgin Mary fell from where it hung on a wall and hit her on the head.

MIRROR IMAGE

The female sex symbol of a cross connected to a circle represents the goddess Venus's hand mirror.

A mirror can cause hallucinations and you can prove this. Turn off the lights in a room so you have just sufficient light to see your reflection in a mirror. Sit approximately one metre away from the mirror, keep as still as you can and concentrate on your face for three minutes or so.   Spooky!

The inventor of roller skates introduced these by skating into a party playing a violin. He lost his balance and crashed into a huge mirror.

A Jewish superstition requires all mirrors in the house to be covered for several days after the death of a loved one. This is because it is believed a mirror will trap the soul of the deceased person and the soul will thus be prevented from moving on to the afterlife.

Although many would argue otherwise, it is not true that your image is reversed when you look in a mirror. You see the right-hand side of your face on the right of the mirror and the left on the left side. A true mirror image.

The superstition that breaking a mirror brings seven years bad luck originates to Roman times. Ancient Romans believed that if you broke a mirror you broke your soul.

MISTLETOE

Mistletoe is only a popular Christmas decoration in Britain.

The custom of kissing under the mistletoe originated in England. A berry had to be be picked from the sprig before someone could be kissed and when all the berries had gone the kissing had to stop.

The name mistletoe, or 'misteltan' as it was called, is derived from two Anglo Saxon words - 'Mistel' meaning dung and 'tan' meaning twig. Or in other words the not very romantic, 'shit on a stick'.

MONEY, MONEY, MONEY

Comedy actor W.C. Fields maintained a very healthy bank account in Germany throughout the Second World War. The reason he gave for this was: 'Just in case the little bastard wins'. (See W.C.)

Florins were originally worth six shillings. Their value didn't drop to two shillings until 1848.

A survey in Oregon, USA, showed that beggars outside Wal-Mart stores could earn more than the people working inside.

British businessman Brian Burnie was so delighted when his wife recovered from breast cancer that he gave away his £16 million fortune to good causes and set up his own cancer charity in 2009. His wife, Shirley, left him because she couldn't cope without their mansion and all that money.

In 1990 'Spy' magazine sent out small denomination cheques to rich celebrities. The value of the cheques got smaller over a period of weeks, the final ones being for only 13 cents. Only two people cashed these, Saudi Arabian arms dealer Adnan Khashoggi and Donald Trump.

In 1999 a six-year-old chimpanzee called Raven was given a set of darts to throw at a list of internet companies. Raven's index was named MonkeyDex. MonkeyDex delivered a 213% gain, outperforming more than 6,000 Wall Street brokers and making Raven the 22nd most successful money manager in the USA.

MUSIC

Mozart once composed a piece requiring both hands and the nose to hit all the notes.

As a child Mozart was terrified by the sound of trumpets.

In 1937 ukuleles were banned in Japan on the grounds that they 'weakened the will of young people.'

There are seventy pieces of wood in a violin.

The world's best-selling musical instrument is the harmonica.

A song you can't get out of your head is called an 'ear worm.'

Emperor Nero ate leeks to improve his singing voice.

Composer Robert Schumann visited an abattoir to plunge his hands into the entrails of dead animals believing this would cure his aches and pains.

On his famous cover of Bob Dylan's 'All Along the Watchtower' Jimi Hendrix plays both lead and bass guitar.

'The Star Spangled Banner' was adopted as the US national anthem in 1931. The previous anthem, 'My Country 'Tis of Thee' was sung to the same melody as 'God Save the Queen.'

Soprano Dame Nellie Melba died from a skin infection following unsuccessful facelift surgery.

The monument to George F. Handel in Westminster Abbey is one of the finest there and includes a full-size statue of the composer. Money for this memorial came from £86,000 left specifically for that purpose in the will of … George F. Handel.

2011 scientific research named Queen's 'We Are the Champions' as the catchiest song ever written.

Collectors of music memorabilia often say they have a lock of hair in their collection certified as coming from the head of composer Franz Liszt. Liszt received so many requests for locks of hair, a collecting craze at the time, that he bought a dog which supplied most of the hair he sent to fans.

N

NAKED AS NATURE INTENDED

A boat capsized in Texas when the sixty passengers all dashed to one side to gawp as they passed a nudist beach.

Topless shopkeepers are legal in Liverpool but only in shops selling tropical fish.

NAME CHANGE

Apache leader Geronimo's actual name was Goyathlay which means 'the yawner.'

'Mary Celeste' was the name of the brigantine famously found in 1872 sailing off the Azores minus her crew.

In 1884 Sir Arthur Conan Doyle published a short story about a survivor from an abandoned ship he named the 'Marie Celeste' and this incorrect name has stuck ever since.

Singer Katy Perry changed her name from Kathryn Hudson to avoid being confused with actress Kate Hudson.

Medieval English surnames no longer in use include; Halfnaked, Swetinbede and Gyldenbollockes.

Cary Elaine Johnson eventually adopted the nickname given to her by friends. Because of her flatulence problem she was likened to a Whoopi Cushion and is now known as Whoopi Goldberg.

Due to a spelling error on her birth certificate Oprah Winfrey's first name is actually Orpah.

The real name of actor/comedian Albert Brooks is Albert Einstein. No need for an explanation why he changed that one!

Stan Laurel of Laurel and Hardy fame was born Stan Jefferson but changed this because it contains an unlucky 13 letters.

Another name change requiring no explanation is Joaquin Phoenix whose birth surname was Bottom.

Gene Simmons of KISS fame was born Chaim Witz.

NATIONAL COSTUME

That length of chord connected around the neck with a metal clip and worn by country music fans is called a bolo tie. The bolo tie is the official item of neckwear in Arizona.

Herero women in Namibia wear a floor-length dress based on clothes they saw worn by German colonists who invaded their country in the early twentieth century.

The Dirndl dress, still worn by older women in Bavaria and Austria and by waitresses in bierkellers, has a knotted belt indicating the wearer's marital status. A knot tied on the left side means she's single, front-centre says she's a virgin and if she's a widow her knot should be at the back.

Lederhosen are the leather shorts worn mostly in Bavaria and by bands in bierkellers. They were originally made for their durability but the most active service they see in the 21st century is catching drips from steins at beer festivals.

The colourful shoes worn by Moroccan men are called babouches.

Salvar are the baggy trousers worn in Turkey.

On 1st August 1746 the Dress Act made the wearing of 'The Highland Dress,' including kilts, illegal in Scotland, Tartan kilts didn't become the official national costume until 1976.

The round hat with flaps, as worn in Russia, is called an ushanka.

The oldest pair of clogs found in Holland date back to 1230.

Vietnamese people wear a conical hat known as a non la. When one of these hats is held up to a light, lines of poetry can be seen written inside the brim.

Japanese kimonos look very exotic to Western eyes but 'kimono' simply means 'the thing worn.'

NEWS

Newsreaders always appeared on BBC television. ITN introduced newscasters.

NIGHTINGALE

Florence Nightingale was born in Florence.

Florence Nightingale carried a pet owl in her pocket. She hand-reared the owl that she had rescued in Athens, she called it Athena.

Florence Nightingale asked that her body be used for medical science and then buried in the nearest convenient burial ground. She also requested that no more than two people should escort her body to its final resting place.

Six uniformed guardsmen carried her undissected body to a grave in the Hampshire cemetery in which her parents are buried.

Cosmetics entrepreneur Elizabeth Arden's real name was Florence Nightingale Graham.

NOBEL

Alfred Nobel, instigator of the Nobel Prize, is well known to be the inventor of dynamite. It is a lesser known fact that his father invented plywood.

NOT AT ALL WELL

A 1995 survey published in the 'Journal of Urology' estimated that 600,000 American men suffered from impotence due to injuries to their crotch area and 40% of these injuries were due to cycling.

In 1992, 5,840 people were treated in American emergency rooms for what were described as 'pillow-related injuries'. Possibly thanks to the confidentiality of medical records, nowhere is it explained whether these injuries were caused by over-energetic pillow fighting, suffocation attempts or some other bedroom activity.

More than two-thirds of bankruptcies in the US are due to medical bills.

Cerumen is the correct name for ear wax.

Actor John Wayne is the first person known to have described cancer as 'The Big C.'

The Greek philosopher Heraclitus tried to cure himself of a serious illness by covering his body in cow dung and allowing it to dry in the sun. He died the following day.

Fried mice were an accepted ancient Egyptian cure for toothache.

NUTS

Ask just about anyone to think of a nut named after a country and they will say 'Brazil'.

In fact Brazil, the country, was named after the nut, not the other way round.

NUTTING

A nutting in the U.K. involves causing injury by bringing the forehead into hard contact with the bridge of a victim's nose.

A-nutting was a German euphemism for love making.

O

ODD BODY PARTS

Despite many pages of written words and hundreds of mentions on the internet I can find no actual evidence that Anne Boleyn had three breasts and an extra finger on her left hand.

Actors Mark Wahlberg and Tilda Swinton and singer Lily Allen have three nipples each. One in eighteen men have an extra nipple and one in fifty women. One Direction singer Harry Styles has two extra nipples. An extra nipple is known as a supernumerary nipple.

Kate Hudson and Halle Berry both have an extra toe on one foot.

Elizabeth Taylor's famous dark eye outlines were not the result of makeup. She had a rare genetic mutation that included double eyelashes.

Ashton Kutcher has webbed feet.

After an early shoot with Marilyn Monroe, then known as Norma Jeane (Not Norma Jean as sung about by Elton John), photographer Joseph Jasgur claimed she had six toes on one foot. This was not true but has become an established urban myth. (See Urban Myths)

Footballer David Beckham has one leg shorter than the other.

In 2013 it was reported that Germany's Wachbatallion soldiers were growing breasts on the left sides of their chests. The condition, known as one-sided gynecomastia, was due to a drill they perform that involves slapping their rifles against the left-side. The constant slapping stimulates hormones, hence the man breasts.

OH NO THEY DIDN'T

Songwriter Irving Berlin couldn't read music.

Humphrey Bogart, a seventh cousin of Princess Diana, always claimed he was born on Christmas Day. His actual birthday was January 23rd but the Warner Brothers Studio thought the Christmas connection would boost his image. (See Bogie)

James Cagney does not say 'You dirty rat' in any of his films. The closest he came to the phrase, immortalised by a thousand impersonators, was in the 1932 movie 'Taxi' when he says: 'You dirty, yellow-bellied rat.'

There is no evidence to suggest Christians were ever forced to fight against gladiators or were fed to wild animals in Rome's Colosseum. The Colosseum did, however, suffer at the hands of Christians who used it as a quarry when building St Peter's and the Vatican.

History books, websites and pub quiz masters insist that Christmas Trees were introduced to Britain and the rest of the world by Germans. It was actually the Brits who introduced Christmas Trees to Germany.

Saint Boniface from Crediton, Devon, discovered the populace of Geismar in Germany worshiping a sacred oak. Boniface cut down the tree, replacing it with a small fir tree as a symbol of Christianity.

Cleopatra is said to have died following a bite from a poisonous asp. Such snakes have never been native to Egypt.

Sir Edwin Landseer is best known for his painting of a stag titled 'Monarch of the Glen.' Generations of cartoonists will be forever in his debt for a painting he made at the age of seventeen of a mountain rescue involving a St Bernard dog with a miniature barrel suspended below its chin. When asked, Landseer said the barrel contained brandy. There is no historical evidence to show St Bernards ever carried mini kegs of brandy in this manner.

OH YES THEY DID

In 1981 Brighton magistrates approved a late bar extension for the annual weekend conference of Alcoholics Anonymous.

In 2013 the Vatican withdrew 6,000 papal medals when someone pointed out they included the word 'Lesus' instead of 'Jesus.'

Pope Francis once worked as a bouncer at a Buenos Aires nightclub.

UK holiday town Southend-on-Sea had to change its new traffic warden uniforms in 2001 after someone pointed out they displayed the logo 'SS'.

Dr Horace Emmett revealed in 1899 that he had discovered the secret of eternal youth which consisted of injections of finely ground squirrel testicles. Dr Emmett died in 1900.

OKLAHOMA

The musical movie 'Oklahoma!' is probably best remembered for the cornfield sequence in which Gordon Macrae sings about the corn being 'as high as an elephant's eye.'

This was filmed in a field of specially grown corn that reached a height of sixteen feet. The average adult elephant's eye is only eight feet above the ground.

OLYMPICS

Up to the 1930s Olympic floor exercises took place with every member of the team on the mat at the same time. Some teams had as many as 100 competitors battling for space.

American athletes have to pay tax on the value of medals won at the Olympics as these are classed as earned income.

The Soviet Union refused to host the 1980 Paralympics claiming the country had no 'invalids'.

Jamaica's 1958 Olympic table tennis champion was eight-year-old Joy Foster.

Croquet was dropped from the Olympics after 1900 when only one spectator turned up.

At the 1976 Montreal Olympics, Nadia Comaneci, aged 14, became the first gymnast to achieve a maximum score. The scoreboard was only capable of showing scores to 9.9 so her perfect ten appeared as 1.00

Javelin throwing was originally an Olympic target sport.

In the 1928 Olympic rowing events an Australian oarsman, Henry Pearce, stopped to allow a family of ducks cross his lane then went on to win the gold medal.

At the 1932 Olympics the 3,000 metres steeplechase was run over a distance of 3,400 metres because an official lost count of how many laps the athletes had covered.

In 1987 North Korea ordered the destruction of a South Korean passenger plane in an attempt to prevent South Korea from staging the Olympics. 115 people died in the tragedy but South Korea went ahead and hosted the Games at Seoul in 1988.

Dental checks were done on athletes at the 2012 London Olympics. 55% of them were found to have tooth decay.

There used to be Olympic medals for Architecture, Sculpture and Statistics.

OPIUM

Opium poppies are said to have first flowered at the spot where Buddha dropped his eyelids after cutting them off so he could never sleep.

6,300 acres of British farmland are given over to growing opium poppies. The main use for these is in the production of morphine for the NHS. Morphine is extracted from the processed seed capsules. A by-product is poppy seeds used on bread and cakes.

ORGANS

Organ donor cards are still shunned by some people who fear their vitals will be whipped out and used for transplant purposes whilst they are still alive but maybe not kicking.

Such worriers can take comfort from the fact that Dr Adrian Upton of McMaster University, Ontario, carried out an electroencephalogram test on a dish of lime jelly and it registered as being alive.

OYSTERS

Oysters have always been a favoured aphrodisiac. The magic ingredient in oysters is dopamine, scientists confirm that dopamine does have an affect on the brain and is very probably a sexual stimulant.

If a suitor doesn't want to go to the expense of oysters a similar quantity of dopamine can be found in brussels sprouts, broad beans and banana peel.

PACKAGE HOLIDAYS

A modern package holiday consists of a flight from a UK airport to a beach resort frequented mostly by Brits, Germans and Russians. Coach transfer from destination airport to hotel will be included and during this your rep will do his or her best to sell you excursions that you can arrange for yourself at half the price. Then, for those who travel abroad but don't like foreigners or foreign food, a buffet of lukewarm Euro pap is available along with the main attraction, an endless booze supply. Although booze is supposedly unlimited some tour companies rely upon package holiday-makers not being too discriminating, preferring quantity to quality. Your gin is more likely to be 'Goblins' than 'Gordons', the vodka 'Aboslut' rather than 'Absolut' and a close examination of the Scotch label will probably show it to be that well-respected brand 'Johnny Wanker'.

All a far cry from the original package holiday organised by a Baptist, Thomas Cook. He arranged a trip to a temperance meeting in Loughborough from Leicester. For one shilling (5p) his customers received the return rail journey and lunch on the train.

Cook progressed to overseas holidays including a 212-day round-the-world trip for 200 guineas. He was the first person to assure holiday-makers they knew the full cost of their trip before leaving home. Everything was included, transport, food and hotel. Unlike modern all-inclusives there was absolutely no alcohol. Thomas Cook's endeavour was to encourage his customers to enjoy educational travel rather than partaking of the demon drink.

PETOMANE

Joseph Pujol (1857-1945) was a French entertainer whose stage name was Le Petomane. The name combines the French verb 'péter', 'to fart' with 'mane', 'maniac'. Or in other words 'farto-maniac'. Puyol was also known as a flatulist.

The best-remembered French stage artist of this era is undoubtedly the actress Sarah Bernhardt, at the height of her career Bernhardt's box office receipts once reached 8,000 Francs, in a single Sunday Le Petomane took 20,000 Francs.

Visitors to Parisian cabaret theatres such as Moulin Rouge were not easily shocked but Le Petomane's act usually got under way with the crowd stunned into silence before their surprise changed to hysterical laughter.

Joseph Pujol farted tunes, his range went from tenor to baritone, and his programme included popular songs of the day, older songs the audience could join in and, it is claimed, impersonations of anyone whose name was shouted out. He put a pipe into his anus and smoked a cigarette through this. His performance climaxed with the blowing out of a candle.

So hilarious was his act that uniformed nurses were stationed around the theatre to aid anyone who collapsed due to laughing too much.

Private, men only, performances took place during which Le Petomane performed sans culottes enabling them to see at close quarters he had nothing hidden in his breeches. The King of Belgium, Leopold II, travelled to Paris to witness one of these legendary performances which began with the star lowering his posterior into a bowl of water, he sucked up the entire contents of the bowl and then expelled this back into the container. He joked that this cleansing reduced the smell that might be expected during the rest of his performance.

Although France, especially Paris, had a reputation back then for ribaldry, Le Petomane's act was such that the press found it difficult to find words to review what he did. Hence his reputation spread mostly by word of mouth.

Asked how long each show lasted Joseph Pujol reportedly said it went on until he 'ran out of breath,' although his ability to do what he did was due to his being able to suck in air then pass it out at will.

Trump is an English word meaning fart.

Scuba divers cannot fart once they get below a depth of 33 feet.

New Zealand's plans to introduce a flatulence tax on animals was dropped after complaints from farmers.

Vegetarians fart more than meat eaters but apparently (I haven't checked this) their farts smell less.

In the 1990s the French developed a pill that made farts smell like chocolate.

Mozart kept a diary of when he broke wind.

'Being married means I can fart and eat ice-cream in bed.' — Brad Pitt

'I have more talent in my smallest fart than you have in your entire body.' — Walter Matthau to Barbra Streisand

The average human farts once per hour.

PETS

In February 2000 a pug named Frodo Baggins became the first animal to hold a U.K. Pet Passport.

Jack Russells are one of the most popular breeds of pet dog all over the world. Devon parson Jack Russell developed his own breed of terrier to be brave, intelligent and able to fit down a fox hole. The flamboyant churchman was a keen follower of the hunt.

A 2014 online survey revealed that 18% of pet lovers slept with their animal.

The above mentioned survey also revealed that 31% of dog owners admitted to talking to their pet on the phone.

Bacteria found on the feet of many dogs has the smell of tortilla chips.

British drivers are legally required to stop if they run over a dog but can drive on if their victim is a cat.

Hitler, Mussolini and Napoleon were all afraid of cats.

A vet in Chile operates a class teaching people how to perform the kiss of life on their dogs.

Queen Elizabeth II took her pet corgi, Susan, on her honeymoon.

The Aboriginal Mbabaram word for dog is 'dog'. A coincidence like this is called a false cognate.

PILGRIM FATHERS

On the fourth Thursday in November our American brothers and sisters stuff themselves with turkey (YouTube has some great clips of Americans setting fire to themselves in attempts to deep-fry whole turkeys) followed by pumpkin pie.

Thanksgiving is in remembrance of a feast held in 1621 when the Pilgrim Fathers entertained Native Americans to three days of seasonal food. Thanksgiving no longer lasts for three days. It is seen as the start of the Holiday Season (what the rest of the world calls Christmas). Since the early 1950s the day after the turkey binge has been known as Black Friday. This is the day when Americans start their Christmas (sorry I mean Holiday) shopping.

Most Americans have a knowledge of geography that ends at the bottom of their yard and a knowledge of history going back as far as the day when Britney Spears chopped off her hair.

Many will tell you the Pilgrim Fathers came from Plymouth and that's as much, or as little as they know.

The Pilgrim Fathers were religious fanatics mostly from Nottinghamshire (that's about 250 miles north of Plymouth) and East Anglia, (350 miles to the east) . Following various debacles in Holland a group set sail in a boat named the Speedwell (formerly the Swiftsure), which they intended keeping in the USA, when they eventually arrived, to use it as a fishing vessel.

It wasn't long before the Speedwell started to take in water so a repair stop was made at Darmouth. Approximately 40 miles along the Devon coast their feet once again started to get wet so they pulled in to Plymouth.

Money from the sale of the leaking Speedwell went towards the purchase of the slightly smaller Mayflower. 102 of the Speedwell's 120 passengers were selected to sail to the US on the Mayflower and the rest, as they say, is history.

Or is it?

When American tourists aren't taking selfies with a copy of a statue of Sir Francis Drake (See Tea Time) they are standing in line on Plymouth's Barbican to take more selfies on the 'historic' Mayflower Steps.

Let us not forget that most of these people have travelled more than 4,000 miles for this unforgettable experience. They will have spent a couple of nights in London taking a ride on the Eye and looking at models of celebrities at Madame Tussaud's. Some will have taken a trip to Edinburgh, which none of them can pronounce, and the others will have boarded coaches for a quick visit to Stonehenge, which none of them know anything about, a photo-op in Stratford-upon-Avon outside the cottage where William Shakespeare probably wasn't born and then on to Plymouth for the Mayflower Steps.

The 'gees' and 'wows' when they see the Steps deter most locals from spoiling their enjoyment by telling them the truth about what they are seeing.

The Doric-style portico above the Steps was erected in 1934, the small stone pier was built approximately a hundred years ago.

Books and knowledgable local residents suggest the seaward side of the Barbican has been rebuilt over the centuries, gradually moving further out into the sea.

If American visitors want to take photographs of the actual spot from which the Pilgrim Fathers set sail my research puts this in the gents toilet at the Admiral MacBride pub.

The Pilgrim Fathers used a product called 'chamber lye'. This was soap produced by allowing urine to mature in a barrel and then mixing this with fat. (See Urine)

PIRATES

When the Governor offered a $500 reward for the capture of the pirate Jean Lafitte, Lafitte issued his own posters offering $5,000 for the capture of the Governor.

English actor Robert Newton filled the role of Long John Silver in a 1950s movie of 'Treasure Island'. Newton had a West Country accent so tended to roll his 'rs' and this has since become the accepted pirate accent. There is no evidence that pirates actually spoke like this although quite a few probably were from the West of England.

Despite international notoriety, Blackbeard (Edward Teach) was only a pirate for two years.

Failure to obey orders could result in pirates being dumped overboard but there is absolutely no evidence to show they ever had to walk the plank. This is yet another Hollywood invention.

Pirates really did pierce their ears and wear heavy earrings. Their reason for this was that it was believed silver and gold could improve the eyesight.

The image of pirates wearing an eye patch is also based on fact. If required to rush out into the dark night to repel boarders the patch could be flicked up and that eye would already be accustomed to the dark.

"Pirates of the Caribbean' movies refer to the 'Pirates Code.' This really existed and was a set of rules established by the captain on each individual ship. The job of a pirate was to steal whatever he could but the Code invariably had a zero tolerance policy when it came to one pirate stealing from another on the same ship with offenders thrown overboard or marooned on an uninhabited island.

Nobody has ever found a genuine pirate's treasure map.

Nelson Mandela's favourite poem was 'Invictus' by William Ernest Henley. Henley was the inspiration for R.L. Stevenson's Long John Silver.

PLACE NAMES

In 2012 residents of a village in Upper Austria were told they could not change the name of their village from Fucking to Fugging as a Fugging already existed in Lower Austria. The mayor of Fugging said his village had also once been called Fucking but now the change had been made two villages could not have the same name.

There's a village called Batman in Turkey.

County Durham in the far north of England boasts a village named Pity Me.

In 2012 the town of Dull in Kinross, Scotland was twinned with Boring, Oregon, USA.

Saint-Louis-du-Ha!-Ha! is in Quebec, Canada.

Dildo is also in Canada.

In 1991 Sexmoan, in the Philippines, had a name change to Sasmuan.

Sandy Balls in the England's New Forest is popular with holiday makers.

In Ohio there are towns called Knockemstiff, Ai, Fly and Three Legs Town.

'Calle Me Falta un Tornillo,' in Valladolid, Spain, translates to English as 'I've Got a Screw Loose Street. There is an IKEA store in this street but it can be hard to find as people keep stealing the street signs.

The Beatles' song 'Penny Lane' takes its name from a Liverpool thoroughfare. (See Beatles) Penny Lanes all over the country take their name from the requirements of the hat industry. Hat makers were supplied with beer at work and when they got home at night they had to collect their urine in a bucket. (See Urine) This was placed outside for collection each morning and workers received a penny for every bucket. The urine was used for treating felt.

PLAYTHINGS

Thanks to the popularity of Happy Meals, McDonald's is the world's largest distributor of toys.

The Stretch Armstrong figure, popular with boys in the 1970s, was filled with corn syrup.

The first Barbie Doll was dressed in a black and white swimsuit. Barbie was introduced in 1959 but didn't smile until 1977.

In 1997 toy manufacturer Mattel launched Share-a-Smile Becky, Barbie's friend who was wheelchair bound. Mattel were praised by disability groups for their introduction of Becky who it was said brought visibility to wheelchair users. Sadly, Becky's wheelchair would not fit through the door of the Barbie Dreamhouse and, if lowered in through the roof, couldn't be squeezed into the house's elevator.

Barbie didn't have a navel until 2000.

After 43 years as a couple Barbie dumped Ken for an Australian surfer called Blaine.

In 2016 a woman officially changed her name to Barbie Dumped Ken after Facebook refused to accept her with this joke name.

The native language of Furbies is Furbish.

POLLS

In recent years pollsters have become the butt of jokes due to their ability to get things very wrong. None of the political polls have got things quite as wrong as the 2003 poll that named footballer David Beckham the fifth most popular Spaniard. The excuse given was that most of the people polled didn't understand the question.

Ted Kennedy and Jimmy Carter's nomination battle was the subject of many opinion polls but the most accurate is recorded as that conducted by disc jockey Cal Bryant.

Bryant took to the airwaves of radio station FGA/AA in the town of Emmetsburg. He asked Carter supporters to flush their toilets, half an hour later he asked Kennedy backers to do the same thing. The level of water in the Emmetsburg water tower dropped almost twelve inches for the winning candidate, it hardly moved for Kennedy. (See Presidential)

POLO

Left-handed people are not permitted to play polo. It is claimed all polar bears are left-handed so would not be allowed on to a polo field.

Polo is recognised as the oldest equestrian team sport having been used as a training game by the Persian army in the sixth century.

The imaginative names given to players on a polo team are; number one, number two, number three and number four.

POO

U.K. television presenter Stuart Hall was jailed in 2013 for sexual offences. Hall had worked on local television before gaining national fame on the TV show 'It's a Knockout' and across Europe for its version of the gameshow 'Jeux Sans Frontieres.'

Not many people know that the disgraced star lost the fortune he invested in a holiday company called Stuart Hall International Travel which didn't look good with its initial letters in bold type on company notepaper.

In Uxbridge, Massachusetts, the police department requested passengers should stop flushing poo when travelling on trains over the city overpass.

Scatomancy is the art of fortune telling by looking at poo.

Pandas can poo fifty times each day. They even eat and poo at the same time.

Hibernating bears can go as long as six months without going to the loo.

During World War II UK troops received a daily allowance of three sheets of toilet paper, Americans got 22.

A common insult in 17th century England was 'You have a turd in your teeth.'

A company called Maximum Performance produces fake poo for testing toilets.

New York City turns out 400 million gallons of raw sewage every year which is approximately the same number of gallons of petrol (gasoline) Americans get through each day.

Cows are looked upon as sacred in India and are allowed to walk the streets unhindered. The streets are remarkably clear of cow dung as this is hand patted into discs that are dried in the sun and used as fuel for cooking in tandoors.

Burger King restaurants in China serve the Mango PooPoo Smoothie.

POST MORTEM

Mausolus, the man who gave his name to mausoleums, died in the fourth century BC. His widow, who was also his sister, had his body cremated, mixed his ashes with water, and drank him.

PRESIDENTIAL

Ulysses S Grant, the man who led the Union armies to bring an end to slavery, was the owner of four slaves.

On 22nd November 1963 Mrs John Connally, wife of the Governor of Texas, greeted John F Kennedy with the words: 'You can't say Dallas hasn't given you a nice welcome.'

Football manager Sir Alex Ferguson collects mementos of J.F.K.'s assassination.

In 1961 a little girl wrote to J.F. Kennedy expressing her distress that Santa was in danger due to Russian nuclear tests. Kennedy replied to say he'd had a word with Santa who was going to be very careful.

William Henry Harrison delivered his inaugural speech as President of the USA on March 4th, 1841 in a violent rain storm. Four weeks later he died of pneumonia.

Thomas Jefferson tied with Aaron Burr in the 1800 US Presidential election. Founding Father Alexander Hamilton used his influence and arranged for Jefferson to be selected by Congress. in 1804 Burr killed Hamilton in a duel.

In 80% of US Presidential elections the tallest candidate wins.

American Independence Day, July 4th, is the day on which Presidents Jefferson, Adams and Monroe all died.

George Washington spent 7% of his annual salary on booze.

Lincoln was suffering from smallpox when he delivered the Gettysburg Address.

Jimmy Carter reported seeing a UFO in Georgia.

Jomo Kenyatta, President of Kenya from 1963 to 1978 can be seen standing behind Paul Robson as an African chief in the movie 'Sanders of the River.'

During his eight-year presidency Bill Clinton only sent two emails. One was to John Glenn on the Space Shuttle and the other was a test because he had doubts the email system worked.

Abraham Lincoln's son, Robert, was saved from being hit by a train by Edwin Booth, brother of John Wilkes Booth who assassinated the President.

PUPPETS

Before he took to eating cookies the Cookie Monster was called Sid.

In Nigeria 'Sesame Street's' Cookie Monster becomes Zobi the Yam Monster. Few Nigerian children have access to cookies so the producers gave Zobi a craving for the country's staple food. His catchphrase is 'Me eat yam.'

There were two pilot shows for 'The Muppets.' 'The Muppets Valentine Show' and 'Sex and Violence.'

Lars Backman was seen by Jim Henson on an edition of 'Good Morning America.' Lars was the inspiration for the Swedish Chef.

Miss Piggy began as a minor character on 'The Muppet Show'.

Statler and Waldorf are named after New York hotels. Waldorf has a wife called Astoria.

The original Kermit looked like a lizard and made his debut in 1955 on 'Sam and Friends'. He had become a frog, made from Henson's mother's coat and two ping-pong balls, when he graduated to 'Sesame Street' in 1969.

Everyone's favourite member of Dr Teeth and the Electric Mayhem is drummer Animal. Although Jim Henson never acknowledged that Animal was based on Keith Moon of the Who one of his 'Fraggle Rock' characters is Wembley, which is where Moon was born.

In a 2015 survey of customers at Travelodge motels Sooty was voted Britain's favourite puppet of all time. Kermit the Frog came second with Gordon the Gopher in third place.

Woody's surname in 'Toy Story' is Pride.

Q

QUOTABLE QUOTES

'If you steal from a single author it's plagiarism, if you steal from many it's research.' — Brian Highley

In 'Grand Hotel' Greta Garbo uttered her most famous movie phrase, 'I vanna be alone.' She maintained this image in real life by failing to turn up for her wedding to co-star John Gilbert.

'I'm an optimist but I'm an optimist who always takes his raincoat.' — Harold Wilson

Trivia buffs have perpetuated the legend that Winston Churchill's 'Fight them on the beaches' speech was actually made by an impersonator called Norman Shelley due to Churchill being too busy fighting the war at the time.

Shelley always denied this and there is no evidence to support the myth. It is also a popular misconception that Churchill said, 'Fight them on the beaches.' He said 'Fight on the beaches,' never using the word 'them'.

Churchill is often misquoted. He never said: 'I have nothing to offer but blood, sweat and tears.' He said: 'I have nothing to offer but blood, toil, tears and sweat.'

'Men occasionally stumble over the truth but most of them pick themselves up and hurry off as if nothing had happened.' — Winston Churchill.

'I don't think President Bush is doing anything about AIDS. In fact, I'm not sure he even knows how to spell AIDS.' — Elizabeth Taylor

'I'm not offended by dumb blonde jokes because I know I'm not dumb and I know I'm not blonde.' — Dolly Parton (See Feet)

'Thank God I'm still an atheist.' — Louis Bunuel

'When a rock star's dead he's made for life.' — Jimi Hendrix

'People say New Yorkers can't get along. Not true. I once saw two complete strangers in New York sharing a cab. One guy took the tyres and the other had the radio and battery.' — David Letterman

'Last week I stated that this woman was the ugliest woman I had ever seen. I have since been visited by her sister and now wish to withdraw that statement.' — Mark Twain

'You can tell German wine from vinegar by the label.' — Mark Twain

RAILWAYS

William Huskisson M.P. was an official guest at the opening of the very first Manchester to Liverpool Railway.

After the official ceremony Huskisson crossed the track to speak to his friend the Duke of Wellington and was struck by George Stephenson's pioneering locomotive, Rocket.

Despite a long career in politics William Huskisson M.P. is only remembered by most trivia geeks as the first person officially listed as having been killed by a train.

REDHEADS

The world's largest sperm bank will not accept donations from redheads as there is insufficient demand.

Prior to losing her hair, Elizabeth I was a redhead. (See Virgin Queen)

Sailors believe that meeting a redhead before starting a journey can lead to disaster.

Redheads are more prone to deafness than those with other colours of hair.

Only 2% of the world's population have red hair. In Eastern Europe the red-haired population is 13%. (See Scots)

Ancient Romans were willing to pay a premium for redheaded slaves.

Religious paintings and stained glass windows often depict Judas Iscariot as a redhead.

Redheads are harder to sedate, they require 20% more anaesthetic than others.

Redheads tend to lose their hair colour later in life than others but they also have a tendency to go straight to white without a grey period.

REFERENCES

Facts in this book have all been triple-checked. Mostly from one hard-copy source, book or newspaper, and in most cases at least two websites. A list of all references would have increased the size and price of the book but doubters can do their own checks via the internet.

RELIGION

Vladimir the Great accepted Orthodox Christianity as the religion of Russia in 987 only after learning that Muslims didn't drink alcohol.

The Bible is the world's best-selling book. About 50 Bibles are sold every minute of every day. (See Biblical)

There are 55 mentions of lions in the Bible.

Jehovah's Witnesses believe that at the end of the world only

144,000 people will be saved. At the last count there were about eight million Jehovah's Witnesses.

Although the concept of being agnostic is many centuries old, that actual word, 'agnostic', was coined in 1860 by Thomas Henry Huxley.

Winston Churchill was a Druid.

The only ideology sanctioned by a government is Juche. Introduced to North Korea in the 1950s by Kim Il-sung who described it as his 'original, brilliant and revolutionary contribution to national and international thought.'

It is estimated that 200 of the mosques in Mecca point in the wrong direction for Muslim's to pray.

People still worship the twelve gods from Greek mythology.

Hinduism is the world's oldest organised religion.

RIDER CLAUSES

A rider clause is the additional clause at the end of a contract demanding extras to be provided in an artist's dressing room. The author worked with many rock bands, some of their demands included: The Police, three new but freshly laundered, white, heavy cotton bathrobes. The Pretenders, eight hot meals that must NOT be from a national fast-food chain. The Damned, twenty four bottles of chilled lager, a bottle of Jack Daniels, a bottle of vodka … with all this in their dressing room they drank tea. Some other weird and wacky riders include:

Coldplay: Eight, stamped local postcards.

Iggy Pop: Seven dwarfs to greet him on arrival. Pizzas to give to the homeless and pre-chopped broccoli to make it easier to throw away.

Status Quo: Marks and Spencer white tube socks. Allegedly they once cancelled a show because these were not provided.

Goldfrapp: One whip or riding crop (not PVC).

James Brown: Hooded hair dryer, iron and ironing board, electric golf cart.

AC/DC: Tea, coffee, sparkling water, Coca-Cola, Sprite, Gatorade, 1 bottle of white wine, 1 bottle of red wine, Bailey's (for drummer Phil Rudd), cheese, raw vegetables, sweets, chewing gum. Proper meal with, for example: salad, mashed potatoes with gravy, sausages or lamb cutlets or beef, custard and cake. Cartons of cigarettes and tobacco so (singer) Brian Johnson can roll his own.

Amy Winehouse: Absolut vodka (must be Absolut), Jack Daniel's, selection of fine beers (for the band), PG Tips teabags, water. Jerk chicken, rice and peas, pizza (margherita), vegetarian and non-vegetarian sandwiches. Doritos, nuts, and bananas. Camel Lights, joss sticks (variety of fragrances), fresh towels, Sign for the door that reads: 'Only Big Boys Can Enter.'

When the author gave Elton John his first major gig in 1970 he turned up with his own supply of brandy, he and his band received a total fee of £75 and his contract had no rider. Since then he has become more demanding with requests for: Six-foot sofa, love seat, easy chairs, table lamps, floor-standing lamps, coffee table, six-foot banqueting table with white linen table cloth, large green plants, arrangement of coloured flowers to include no chrysanthemums, lilies, carnations or daisies.

Van Halen had what was almost certainly the most famous rider of all time. They requested a bowl of M&Ms with all the brown ones removed. David Lee Roth said this was included in their list of demands just to make sure the promoter had read the contract. If the bowl of M&Ms, minus brown, were not on the dressing room catering table the band would find the venue in breach of contract, cancel the show and expect to be paid in full.

Things have changed considerably since the Beatles asked for a black and white television and a few Coca-Colas. Elvis Presley's modest early needs called for ten soft drinks and a glass of water.

RIVERS

So much fresh water is driven into the Atlantic from the Amazon River that surface water can be drinkable up to 200 miles from shore.

By volume of water, the Amazon is bigger than the next seven largest rivers combined.

The Imjin River in South Korea is known as 'river of the dead' because large numbers of bodies from North Korea wash down it.

48.7% of all the land in the world drains its water into the Atlantic.

The flow of the Chicago River was reversed by engineers in the early 1900s to prevent sewage from flowing into Lake Michigan and it still flows in the wrong direction.

ROADRUNNER

The roadrunner is a member of the cuckoo family.

The roadrunner is the national bird of Mexico.

ROAD RUNNER

Wile E. Coyote, who, at the time of writing has starred in 49 cinema and TV cartoons chasing Road Runner, also appeared in five shorts as an antagonist of Bugs Bunny. In the 'Road Runner' shows the Coyote is usually silent but in the Bugs Bunny outings he speaks with a refined accent provided by Mel Blanc. (See Foody Fads)

Wile. E Coyote appears to obtain his Road Runner-catching gadgets without sending payments to the Acme mail-order company. However, in the 2003 cartoon 'Back in Action' it is revealed that the coyote works for Acme. In an earlier outing he also mentions he has a protege called Calamity Coyote who owns an unlimited Acme credit card.

In the 'Family Guy' episode 'I Never Met the Dead Man' Wile E. Coyote is in a car driven by Peter Griffin that runs over Road Runner. Peter asks if he hit 'that ostrich' and Wile tells him to keep going.

ROBIN HOOD

The tourist industry of Nottinghamshire relies heavily on the county's connection with Robin Hood. Although Robert Fitzooth, Earl of Huntingdon, (a fictitious identity for Robin) was allegedly born in Nottinghamshire, history suggests that Robin and his Merry Men were based in Yorkshire.

Robin Hood Airport serves Sheffield and Doncaster in Yorkshire.

In the 16th century May Day was known as Robin Hood Day.

The Miller and Carter Steak House (formerly the Three Nuns) in Mirfield, Yorkshire hides an interesting secret. Not far from the pub stands Kirklees Abbey, legend has it that Robin Hood fired an arrow from his deathbed on the upper floor of the Abbey with instructions to his followers that he should be buried where the arrow landed. Robin's cousin, the prioress of Kirklees, had arranged blood letting to cure a sickness from which Robin was suffering and it isn't clear whether she purposely or accidentally allowed him to bleed to death.

Behind the pub is what appears to be a grave with an epitaph dedicated to 'Robert Earl of Huntingtun' who apparently died in 'Dekembris 1247.' This all ties in perfectly with the Robin Hood legend. However, the inscription was made when the 'grave' was restored in 1850 and a TV documentary found no indication of ground disturbance as there would be for a grave. Ground penetrating radar found no trace of human remains.

Robin Hood's closest ally is said to have been Little John, ironically named because of his gigantic stature. It is claimed that John was with Robin on the day he died. Little John is said to be buried under the branches of a yew tree in St Michael's churchyard, Hathersage, Derbyshire where he died in a cottage close to the church..

The inscription on this grave reads: 'Here lies buried Little John the friend and lieutenant of Robin Hood.' The grave is indeed beneath a yew tree.

In 1784 Captain James Shuttleworth led the exhumation of this grave where he found the skeleton of a man over seven feet tall.

ROBOTS

'Robot' was first used in the play 'R.U.R' ('Rossum's Universal Robots'). The word comes from the Czech word 'robota' which means 'drudgery.'

'Android' refers only to robots that look male, feminine robots are 'Gyroid.'

The world now employs more than a million industrial robots, half of these are in Japan.

'Spirit' and 'Opportunity', the robots on Mars, were only built to last 90 days. They were still trudging around after three years during which they covered 10.5 miles. The cables powering the drilling mechanisms on both Mars rovers were protected by shields made from metal taken from the ruins of the World Trade Centre.

The only character to appear unchanged in all six 'Star Wars' movies is R2-D2.

The world's first humanoid robot, Elektro, made his debut in 1939. The seven-foot-tall machine walked and had 700 words stored on 78rpm discs. Things went steadily downhill and in 1960 Elektro appeared in the B-movie 'Sex Kittens Go to College.'

ROCK ON

Bob Dylan's recording debut was as support harmonica player on calypso singer Harry Belafonte's 'Midnight Special' album.

The YMCA dropped plans to sue pop band the Village People over their 'YMCA' hit record when it became clear the song was resulting in a massive boost to membership applications.

Willie Nelson claims he smoked a joint on the White House roof while Secret Service kept guard.

Keith Richards claims he was fast asleep, woke up in the middle of the night and recorded 30 seconds of what would become the iconic guitar riff for '(I Can't Get No') Satisfaction.' (See Rolling Stones)

Bob Marley was buried with his Gibson guitar, a Bible open at the 23rd Psalm and a bud of marijuana.

ROLLING STONES

The author of this book wrote questions and answers for many editions of Trivial Pursuit include the 'Rolling Stones Collector's Edition'. The credits provided with the game give Brian Highley superior billing over former Stones guitarist Bill Wyman who helped edit the questions and answers.

President John F. Kennedy was a student at the London School of Economics as was Mick Jagger, but not at the same time.

Andy Warhol is frequently credited with devising the Rolling Stones' tongue and lips logo, voted the world's greatest band logo in a 2008 online poll.

The logo first appeared on the sleeve of the 1969 'Sticky Fingers' album and was actually devised by English graphic designer John Pasche.

'I think Mick Jagger would be astounded and amazed if he realised to how many people he is not a sex symbol but a mother image.' — David Bowie

'I've never had a problem with drugs. I've had problems with the police.' — Keith Richards

'Whatever side I take I know I'll be blamed.' — Keith Richards

'I love his work but I couldn't warm to him even if I was cremated next to him.' — Keith Richards on Chuck Berry

ROYAL BOX

Drury Lane Theatre in London has a King's Side and a Prince's Side. This is due to the fact that George III and his son the Prince of Wales (later George IV) spent so much time fighting that they were always kept well apart in the theatre so as not to spoil the performance for the rest of the audience. (See Mad King)

King Archimadus of Sparta was fined for marrying a short woman. Officials believed the tiny Queen would give birth to 'Kinglets' rather than fully-grown Kings.

Edward III ordered his chefs to prepare a luxurious Christmas dinner in 1350 for the Kings of Scotland and France. Both were locked in his dungeons at the time.

Edward VIII, the Duke of Windsor, had steps constructed to enable Cora, his rheumatic cairn terrier, to climb into his bed. (See Pets)

George V died on a very cold day in January 1936. When his body was moved to the chapel where it would lie in state his son, Edward VIII went out to follow the cortege without a coat. His mistress, Mrs Wallis Simpson, handed him one of his father's coats to keep him warm and he wore this during the sombre procession. On arrival at the church Edward found a note in the pocket in the KIng's writing. It read: 'Red Romany, 3.30 Brighton.'

The King had fallen ill before being able to place a bet on the horse which had won the race at odds of eight to one.

Katherine, Queen of Valois, was buried in Westminster Abbey in 1437. Sadly her grave stood in the way of Henry VII when he came to build his famous chapel.

The Queen was unceremoniously dug up and her coffin was placed at the side of her husband's tomb where it remained for over three hundred years.

Fashionable members of society paid a few pence to the clergy for a view of Katherine's remains. Samuel Pepys wrote about his visit in his famed diary : 'I had the upper part of her body in my hands and I did kiss her mouth, reflecting upon it that I did kiss a Queene.'

Anne Boleyn is the only British monarch to have been beheaded with a sword.

George IV had so much to drink on his wedding day he passed out on the floor.

Princess Marina, Duchess of Kent, was the first member of any Royal Family to appear on television. She stood in front of Baird's experimental equipment in1935.

Queen Elizabeth II has a special shelf built into her Rolls-Royce for her handbag.

The parrot mascot on HMS Lancaster, a Royal Navy ship, was always taken ashore during royal visits due to its habit of shouting 'Show us your tits.'

Princess Diana described the Royal Family as 'a leper colony.'

'I'm as thick as a plank.' — Princess Diana

The great and the good of Vancouver, Canada, gathered in 2010 to see Prince Philip, consort of Elizabeth II, open the annexe to their City Hall. His speech consisted of: 'I declare this thing open, whatever it is.'

'How do you keep the natives off the booze long enough to get them to pass the test?' — Prince Philip to a driving instructor in Scotland.

'It looks as if it was put in by an Indian.' — Prince Philip, looking at a badly wired fuse box while touring an Edinburgh factory in 1993

'I couldn't believe it the other day when I picked up a British newspaper and read that 82 per cent of men would rather sleep with a goat than me.' — Sarah Ferguson

RULERS

John Davis Murray was a perfectly ordinary engineer who was sent by the British Phosphate Mining and Shipping Company to manage their mines on Christmas Island.

It was essential for Murray to have full co-operation from the native work-force so the company guaranteed him such support by having him declared King.

From 1891 to 1910 Murray had full power over the island. He then made a return visit to London and was forced to abdicate after falling in love with a woman who refused to take on the title and duties of Queen.

Queen Anne, 1165-1714, outlived all 17 of her children.

Margaret Beaufort, 1443-1509 was the mother of Henry VII and as such is recognised as the matriarch of all European royalty. The current heirs to the British throne are her direct ancestors.

Members of the public could purchase tickets to watch George II and his Queen eating dinner.

King Alfonso of Spain, 1886-1931, employed an Anthem Man. The King was so tone deaf he needed someone to tell him when the national anthem was played so he knew to stand up.

Queen Isabella of Spain, 1451-1504, bathed only twice in her entire life. (See Virgin Queen)

Charles VII of Sweden was assassinated in 1167. It is still a mystery why he was Charles VII as there had never been Charles I, II, III, IV, V or VI.

SALT

If all the salt in all the oceans and seas was spread evenly across all the land it would be 500 feet deep.

The only working salt mine remaining in Britain is at Winford near Norwich, it produces rock salt to spread on roads during the winter.

Because of their natural cleanliness and constant temperature of 14C salt mines are often used for storage. Although never officially made public it is generally believed that during World War II the Crown Jewels were stored in the Winford salt mine.

It is a commonly believed fallacy that the word salary comes from Roman soldiers having been paid in salt. Roman soldiers were paid cash like everyone else.

The only thing whales can taste is salt.

Salt can be deadly. A single gram of salt for each kilogram of your weight will kill you and was a ritual form of suicide in China.

SCAMS

Many houses in Nigeria have 'This House Not For Sale' painted on their walls. This is because a local scam involves waiting until people go out then obtaining a deposit from unsuspecting members of the public to whom the scammers 'sell' the house.

In 1916 Louis Enricht offered the opportunity to invest in his company producing a substitute for gasoline (petrol). Reporters were invited to his New York home where one of them was invited to add a green pill (he warned it was deadly poisonous) into a bucket of water and this was poured into the tank of a car. The vehicle started immediately and all those present wrote glowing reports.

Henry Ford sent Enricht a cheque for $10,000 development costs. Ford was allegedly infuriated when his cheque was returned because inventor Hiram Maxim had offered much more. Eventually a banker handed over $100,000, as security he was given a sealed envelope containing the 'secret' of the new miracle fuel.

It didn't take long for experts to work out that the fuel did drive a car but it was a mixture of acetone (nail polish remover), acetylene and water. It cost more than petrol and eventually it corroded a car's engine beyond repair.

At the age of 75 Enricht gave up his green pill scam and launched a new fuel, based on distilled peat.

Backers were quick to support this new project but it was soon realised investors' money was being syphoned into Enricht's personal account. He was arrested for grand larceny. He demonstrated his peat distillation equipment to the jury but it was revealed that an underground tank of gasoline was supplying the flow of fuel through the peat.

He was sentenced to 3 to 7 years in Sing Sing and was released as a very sick man after two years.

Everybody should now know to avoid the email that arrives,

often from Nigeria, from the guy who needs to put a million into your bank account to transfer it out of the country but you have to pay up-front bank charges. Phishing is another internet scam whereby you receive an email from your bank or credit card provider warning there's a problem with your account. If you open the link you see a fake version of your bank's Website where you are asked to type in your details or the account will be suspended.

You have just given your details to a scammer who is already using the information you provided to rob you.

US circus owner P.T. Barnum noticed that people were creating queues by spending too long in front of each exhibit in the circus menagerie. He erected a large arrow with the message, 'THIS WAY TO THE EGRESS.' Visitors didn't realise 'egress' was an alternative word for 'exit' and cheerfully left the menagerie thinking they were about to view some exotic breed of bird.

There are those out there still sending deposits to the 'Work at home and earn a fortune' scam. The scammers really are making a fortune working from home by taking your money and giving nothing back.

Signed copies of Buddy Holly's Greatest Hits album still occasionally turn up on internet auction sites. The album was first released in 1996. Buddy Holly died in 1959. (See Afternoon T/V)

In the early 1900s a Miss Louisa Miles would invite upmarket jewellers to bring selections of diamonds, rubies, emeralds and gold to an expensive Mayfair mansion. She said she was Constance Brown, housekeeper to the mega-rich Lady Campbell. When the jeweller arrived he would undoubtedly have been impressed by the luxury of the house and would have had few qualms when the 'housekeeper' explained that Lady Campbell was ill in bed so please could she take the selection of jewels to her for her to make her selection.

It wouldn't be long before the jeweller realised there was total silence from the bedroom. His attempts to open the door proved it to be locked. Louisa had long gone, taking the expensive samples with her, out through the bedroom window of the apartment she had rented for the day.

There are those who still fall for the Perfect Girlfriend scam on the internet. You are sent a stock photo of a gorgeous girl and she agrees to a date after exchanging a few emails. Of course she needs you to send her the cash for her transport to your agreed venue and a hotel room and she'll also go for the sympathy vote by asking if you can help with her rent.

Of course she doesn't show up for the date because she doesn't exist.

SCHOOL

Paris Hilton's mother went to school with Janet Jackson.

Tom Cruise had attended fifteen different schools by the time he was fourteen.

Russian children start school on September 1st even if it falls at the weekend. This is known as 'Knowledge Day' marking the first day of their education and the first day of Autumn.

Dutch kids start school on their fourth birthday, resulting in the chaos of pupils arriving one at a time through the year.

Many Japanese schools don't employ cleaners. The children do the cleaning as part of a Buddhist practice associating cleanliness with morality.

The longest school holiday in Australia is the Christmas holiday which falls during the Australian summer.

SCOTS

In 2007 Scotland paid £125,000 to find a new national slogan. The winner was 'Welcome to Scotland.'

Pontius Pilate who presided at the trail of Jesus was born in Scotland.

US astronauts use notebooks fireproofed with a material produced out of seaweed obtained from the Isle of Lewis.

Scotland boasts the world's shortest commercial flight. The journey from Westray to Papa Westray in Orkney is a distance of 1.5 miles and takes 47 seconds.

Everyone has heard of the Loch Ness Monster but how many know about claims of sightings of Morag, a mermaid, in Lake Morar.

In the movie 'Braveheart' this is the nickname of William Wallace. In reality Braveheart was the nickname of Robert the Bruce.

Scotland really does have more ginger-haired people than anywhere else. Around 13% of the population have red hair. (See Redheads)

South East Scotland also breaks another record with 57% of the population having blue eyes.

Glasgow claims to have more stretched limos than Los Angeles. (See L.A.)

SERIAL KILLERS

In January 2007 German police were frantically searching for the Phantom of Heilbronn, a woman whose DNA had been found on objects at the scenes of 39 murders. It took until March for them to realise they were collecting samples on swabs contaminated with the DNA of a female factory worker at the swab factory in Austria.

The most prolific serial killer in modern history is regarded to be Dr Harold Shipman. The British doctor murdered over 250 of his patients. He hung himself in his prison cell in 2004, one day before his 58th birthday.

In his book, 'Murder Among Us,' Steven Egger claims that serial killers frequently had an unusual or unnatural relationship with their mothers.

Almost all serial killers confess to gaining pleasure by torturing small animals before going on to killing humans.

Most psychiatrists agree that serial killers cannot be cured of their obsession.

76% of the world's serial killings are in the USA, Europe comes second with 17%. California has the highest number of America's serial killers with 16% of the national total and Maine is at the bottom with zero.

84% of America's serial killers are Caucasian.

Less than 10% of serial killers are female but women and girls constitute 65% of victims.

SEVEN YEAR ITCH

Marriages are often said to face difficulties in their seventh year. A 2014 study of this phenomenon discovered that this was the time when many wedding gifts reached the end of their useful life and the couple's budget comes under strain due to the requirement to replace everything.

SEXUAL EQUALITY

Ancient Greek philosopher Aristotle believed everyone should be loved according to their worth. Hence, he said, wives should love their husbands more because men are superior.

The term spinster originates from the belief that the ability to spin wool or linen was the main attribute required to become a wife. A girl was not considered to be worthy of marriage until she had spun sufficient thread to produce the cloth to create her entire trousseau. Hence, a spinster was a woman still trying to spin enough to stock her bridal trunk.

Some tribes in Africa observed a custom to fatten up brides prior to their wedding to make them unattractive to other tribesmen.

It was traditional for Hungarian brides to wear as many as twenty petticoats beneath their wedding dress.

'It is a woman's business to get married as soon as possible and a man's to keep unmarried as long as he can.' — George Bernard Shaw 'Man and Superman'

Despite what most men may think, Charles Darwin maintained that for most species it is the female who chooses her mate from the males available.

'No doubt exists that all women are crazy; it's only a question of degree.' — W.C. Fields (See W.C.)

'I'd rather have two girls at 21 each than one at 42.' — W.C. Fields

'Never try to impress a woman because if you do she'll expect you to keep up the standard for the rest of your life.' — W.C. Fields

SHAKESPEARE

William Shakespeare is an anagram of 'I am a weakfish speller.'

There are more than 80 variations of the way Shakespeare's name was spelled. There is no record of him ever having used the spelling that has now become accepted as correct.

William Shakespeare was baptised on April 26th 1564 when it was traditional for baptism to take place three days after birth, making his birthdate 23rd April. He died on 23rd April 1616 and it is generally accepted he was born on and died on St George's Day. However, at the time of Shakespeare's birth Britain still adhered to the old Julian Calendar, the Gregorian Calendar was not introduced until 1582. What was April 23rd when Shakespeare was born would be May 3rd on today's calendar.

The Moons of Uranus are named after Shakespeare's characters.

Shakespeare is commonly referred to as an 'Elizabethan Playwright.' Most of his plays were written after the death of Elizabeth so he is more accurately described as a 'Jacobean Playwright.'

William Arden, a relative of Shakespeare on his mother's side, was arrested for taking part in a plot against Elizabeth I. He was imprisoned in the Tower of London prior to execution.

The only two plays Shakespeare wrote entirely in verse are 'Richard II' and 'King John'.

When Shakespeare married Anne Hathaway he was 18, she was 26 and three months pregnant.

Shakespeare never published any of his plays.

None of the characters in Shakespeare's plays are smokers.

In addition to writing 37 plays and 154 sonnets, Shakespeare also found time to act and took part many times in his own plays.

Shakespeare's original grave marker in Holy Trinity Church, Stratford-upon-Avon, depicted him holding a bag of grain. His followers had this replaced with a quill.

In 1890 Eugene Schiffelin embarked on a project to introduce every bird mentioned in Shakespeare's works to the USA. He released 60 starlings in New York's Central Park. There are now an estimated 200 million starlings in America.

SHARING

There are only two things a child will share willingly - communicable diseases and his mother's age. — Dr Benjamin Spock.

SIMPSON QUOTES

'I'd be mortified if someone ever made a lousy product with the Simpson name on it.' — Lisa Simpson

'Hi, I'm Troy McClure. You might remember me from such self-help videos as 'Smoke Yourself Thin' and 'Get Confident, Stupid.' — Troy McClure

'Remember the time when you ate my goldfish and you lied to me and said I never had any goldfish. Then why did I have the bowl, Bart? Why did I have the bowl?' — Milhouse Van Houten

'I'd rather let a thousand guilty men go free than chase after them.' — Chief Wiggum

'I used to be with it but then they changed what 'it' was and now what I'm with isn't 'it'. And that's why 'it' seems weird and scary to me.' — Grampa Simpson

'This is one thousand monkeys working at a thousand typewriters. Soon they'll have written the greatest novel known to man. Let's see. 'It was the best of times it was the blurst of times.' You stupid monkey.' — Mr Burns

'Me fail English? That's unpossible.' — Ralph Wiggum

'Aren't we forgetting the true meaning of Christmas: the birth of Santa.?' — Bart Simpson

'Alcohol and night swimming. It's the perfect combination.' — Lenny

'Oops, lost a nail. Well that's leprosy for you.' — Mr Burns

'I don't mind if you pee in the shower but only if you're taking a shower.' — Marge Simpson

'Ladies and gentlemen, what you are seeing is a total disregard for the things St. Patrick's Day stands for. All this drinking, violence, destruction of property. Are these the things we think of when we think of the Irish?' — Kent Brockman

(See Homer Simpson Wit and Wisdom)

SKIN

The skin is the human body's largest organ.

In an average day we inhale 700,00 of our own skin flakes.

The term for skin peeling, as after sunbathing, is 'desquamation.'

There are over 1,000 species of bacteria growing on the average person's skin and around 20 species of fungus between the toes.

Between 20,000 and 50,000 years ago everybody was black. Lighter skin pigments developed as people moved to colder climates causing a loss of melanin pigment.

SING ALONG

The earliest known English song , 'Summer Is Acumen In,' is variously attributed to John of Fornsete, a monk from Reading, or W. de Wycombe who worked as a scribe for some time at St Andrews in Worcester.

SNOW

Various sources claim there are between 20 and 50 different words for 'snow' in the 'Eskimo language.'

There is no such thing as the Eskimo language, there are a number of languages that can be referred to as 'Eskimo'.

All Inuit languages, except for West Greenlandic, have only three basic words for snow. Qaniy - falling snow. Aniyu - fallen snow. Alun - snow on the ground.

Chionophobia is a persistent fear of snow or of being trapped by snow. (See Ale and Hearty)

On 18th February 1979 it snowed in the Sahara Desert.

A well known book of records claims that on January 28th 1887 a snowflake fell in Fort Keogh, Montana that was 15 inches wide and eight inches thick.

SOUVENIRS

When Mel Gibson's movie 'The Passion of Christ' became an unexpected box office smash hit, replicas of crucifixion nails went on sale across the USA at a price of $10 each.

The gun that killed Jesse James, the outlaw, sold at auction in 2003 for £218,750.

SPACE PIONEERS

Soviet authorities claimed Laika, the first dog in space, was painlessly euthanised after six days in space. The news later leaked that Laika had, in fact, died just six hours into the flight due to a faulty temperature control system.

When Apollo astronauts were asked to choose one of three sizes of sleeve required to connect to a system for urinating in space they invariably claimed to be large. NASA entered into the spirit by renaming the sizes 'Large,' 'Gigantic' and 'Humungous.'

Apollo 8 was a precursor for the eventual Moon landing. It didn't go as well as reported. Astronaut Frank Borman suffered from severe sickness and diarrhoea, the globules floated around the inside of the ship in zero gravity and had to be cleaned up by the other two astronauts, James Lovell and William Anders. Although this incident was not publicised and Borman asked his fellow-astronauts to keep the matter a secret they talked him into reporting his illness to NASA.

When Alan Shephard turned up for training in 1959 he was pictured in newspapers and magazines standing next to his 1957 Corvette. Recognising the publicity to be gained from a connection with heroic astronauts, General Motors offered them all a new car for minimal lease terms.

When Alan Shephard was waiting for blast-off a reporter asked him what he was thinking about. He replied: 'The fact that every part of this shit was built by the lowest bidder.'

During the first Space Station project involving both US and Russians the astronauts (American) fell out with the cosmonauts (Russian) over toilet facilities. There are two bathrooms on the Space Shuttle and people usually used the closest but the rich diet enjoyed by the Russians had a tendency to block the loo so the Americans decided upon 'ours' and 'theirs' facilities.

SPEED LIMITS

A frightened limpet can dash away from danger at a speed of two miles per hour.

In a dive the peregrine falcon can reach a speed of 200 mph.

The Atlantic sailfish has clocked up 68 mph in water. The top speed of a dolphin is 37 mph.

The Australian Dragon Fly is the world's fastest insect, reaching speeds up to 35 mph. (See Insects)

The sound heard when a whip is cracked is the tip of the chord breaking the sound barrier.

The Chilean word 'achaplinarse' means to run around in the fashion of Charlie Chaplin's little tramp character.

Usain Bolt was heralded the fastest man on Earth but human footprints discovered in Australia were dated back 20,000 years and measurements showed the person to have been running at 23 mph. Bolt's fastest race peaked at a speed of 27.44 mph.

Woodpeckers can peck 20 times a second.

The Earth orbits the Sun at a speed of 67,062 mph.

Bulls can run faster uphill than down.

SPIDERS

A 2015 report claims that during a lifetime the average human consumes eight spiders whilst asleep. (See Insects)

SPORT

'Baseball has the great advantage over cricket of being sooner ended.' — George Bernard Shaw

In the early days of women's cricket blue balls were used so that players did not become overexcited by the usual red ones.

Pink balls were first introduced to men's cricket in 2017 because they showed up better than red ones during floodlit evening matches.

'The trouble with my golf game is that I stand too close to the ball after I've hit it.' — Jack Benny

In the 1988 Calgary Olympics ski jump Eddie - The Eagle - Edwards came last in his two events, 70m jump and 55m jump. At the time he was the British champion.

Even regular golfers will tell you a golf ball has 360 dimples. In fact there is no regulation number of dimples and modern golf balls have anywhere between 350 and 500.

A 2009 Belgian bodybuilding competition was cancelled after a pre-contest drugs test was announced and all the competitors inexplicably dropped out.

STRONG AND STABLE

In 1970, just before he became Secretary of State for Social Services in Edward Heath's government, Sir Keith Joseph proved his ability for the job by announcing: 'It needs to be said that the poor are poor because they don't have enough money.'

SUBMARINES

In exchange for Pepsi products, Russia gave the company 17 submarines, a cruiser, a frigate and a destroyer. It was the world's 7th largest submarine fleet at the time.

Nuclear and diesel-powered submarines are equipped with a snorkel to draw air from the surface while submerged.

Women were not permitted to serve on Royal Navy submarines until 2011.

In 1864 during the American Civil War the 'H.L. Hunley' became the first submarine to sink an enemy ship.

'Yellow Submarine' by the Beatles is the only UK chart-topper with 'Submarine' in its title. (See Beatles)

SUN

A pinhead-sized sample from the core of the Sun would be so hot it could kill someone a hundred miles away.

1.3 million Earths would fit inside the Sun.

The Sun rotates on its axis once every 25.38 Earth days.

The Sun consumes four million tons of hydrogen every second.

From the time it was discovered to the time it was downgraded from full planet status, Pluto did not complete a single orbit of the Sun.

99.85% of the Solar System's mass is in the Sun.

SURREAL

Surrealist artist Salvador Dali believed he was the reincarnation of his dead brother.

Dali always said that when his wife, Gala, died he would eat her. He fully intended to carry out this promise but was talked out of it by friends.

In 2017 the body of Salvador Dali was exhumed so that DNA samples could be taken to settle a paternity case. Witnesses of the exhumation reported his trademark moustache was still in place.

Tarot card reader Maria Pilar Abel Martinez claimed her mother had a liaison with Dali in 1999. She says her physical resemblance to the artist is so strong 'the only thing I'm missing is the moustache.' Her supposed paternal grandmother had told her, 'I know you're not my son's daughter and that you are the daughter of a great painter.' She also noted that her granddaughter was 'Odd, just like your father.'

If the DNA had matched Pilar would have been heir to a quarter of Salvador Dali's fortune. There was no match.

T

TALE OF TWO ACCENTS

I spent the first thirty years of my life in West Yorkshire. When I return to my old home-county friends and colleagues from several decades ago remark on my 'posh accent'. Those in my adopted county of Devon think it hilarious to mock me with cries of 'E ba gum,' oblivious to the fact that their own accents make them sound like extras in a pirate movie. (Incidentally Robert Mugabe, President of Zimbabwe, has allegedly had people shot for pointing out that his surname is 'E ba gum' backwards.)

In the 1980s it was reported that Her Majesty the Queen no longer uses the Queen's English. I always thought the Queen's English was the classless, non-regional accent spoken by my three kids, all born in Devon but probably more influenced by TV than by the local farmers and their offspring. The Queen speaks her own version of English where 'off' becomes 'orf', 'really' is 'rarely' and 'mine' is 'one's.'

Accents come into and go out of fashion. TV and radio commercials provide a good reflection of what's 'in'. Polls reveal that, for no discernible reason, listeners go through periods of trusting different accents from around the U.K.

For a period of some twelve months I boosted my income quite considerably as a voice-over on commercials when everyone would buy anything off someone with a Yorkshire accent. I sold beer, cars, and ice-cream. I was 'the voice' of a discount clothing store who insisted that for one commercial I announced, 'Pierre Cardin suits only £45, at this price they won't last long.' Most bizarrely of all I was called upon to employ my east of the Pennines pronunciation to plug a country life park displaying the history of Devon farms and traditional crafts.

Overnight work dried up for me as a Liverpool accent became trustworthy, this was replaced by Geordie. Scottish accents were briefly en vogue until it was pointed out that when listeners heard these commercials they visualised little Jimmy Krankie, which wasn't the required image for most products, and Welsh accents have never sold anything to the east of Offa's Dyke. (See Barriers)

Tourists hearing me in my local pub often ask what part of Lancashire I'm from. This always leads to jokes about the best thing ever to come out of Lancashire being the M62 and they then show their lack of historical knowledge by mentioning the War of the Roses which they clearly think was a skirmish fought somewhere near Todmorden between Yorkshiremen and Lancastrians bashing one another over the head with white and red roses.

TATTOOS

Often spelled 'tatoo', the word 'tattoo' is one of the most regularly misspelled in the English language.

In the 19th century sailors believed that by having a pig tattooed on one foot and a cockerel on the other they would prevent drowning.

A 2012 survey revealed that in the USA more women (23%) had tattoos than men (19%).

Due to variations in the skin, tattoos on joints and the feet fade more quickly.

The area of skin where a tattoo has faded during healing, or where the tattooist has accidentally missed a section, is known in the trade as a 'holiday'.

Tattoo designs displayed in shops for clients to choose from are known as 'flash'.

In 1909 naked lady tattoos were banned in the US Navy.

Most tattoo artists now offer 'invisible' tattoos using UV sensitive ink. These cannot be seen except under UV lighting as in a club.

Tattoo armbands became popular in the 1990s after Pamela Anderson was pictured with a barbed-wire tattoo around her arm.

Fashion designer Marc Jacobs has a SpongeBob SquarePants tattoo.

Temporary henna tattoos can cause permanent scarring.

TAXING

'The hardest thing in the world to understand is the income tax.' — Albert Einstein

Everyone's tax returns are public in Sweden, Finland and Norway.

One of several reasons for the French Revolution was the introduction of a tax on salt. (See Salt)

The US Civil War was partly over slavery but mainly about taxation.

In 2012 a theatre in Catalonia started selling patrons carrots instead of tickets as a protest against a 13% rise in VAT on cultural activities in Spain. The VAT on a theatre visit went up from 8% to 21%. Drama enthusiasts who purchased a carrot (VAT 4%) were then given free entrance to the theatre. The manager said he had considered lettuces but thought these too bulky to sit with through a performance. Another suggestion was for tomatoes but he envisaged these being thrown at the cast.

Lady Godiva's famed naked horse ride through Coventry was a tax protest.

Roman emperor Vespasian introduced a tax on urine during the first century AD. Urine had multiple uses including tanning and laundering. (See Urine)

Broadsheet newspapers are that same, massive, unmanageable

size around the world thanks to a tax introduced in England in 1816. The so-called 'knowledge tax' was levied according to the number of pages so newspaper publishers introduced broadsheet to accommodate more text on fewer pages.

Peter the Great introduced a beard tax in Russia in 1705.

Much of Elizabeth I's popularity in England was thanks to her low tax policies. (See Virgin Queen)

Many old buildings in England still have blocked up windows following the introduction of the Window Tax in 1691.

Canada raised $23 million between the 1880s and 1923 from a Chinese Head Tax. Chinese immigrants were taxed in an attempt to discourage them from entering the country on the newly constructed Canadian Pacific Railway.

TEA TIME

In 1981 Yorkshire cricketer Geoff Boycott walked off the field at Trent Bridge on the fourth day of the First Test against Australia. When asked why he hadn't waited for the official tea interval Boycott explained that, like Her Majesty the Queen, he always took tea at four on a Sunday.

Cricket is the only international sport with an official tea interval which probably accounts for the lack of interest in cricket in the USA.

Americans cannot make tea. Tea in America is invariably served iced from a can. Although this beverage is virtually without flavour it is a safer option than asking for 'hot tea'. My wife ordered 'hot tea' in premises ranging from truck stops, through what Americans refer to as 'high end restaurants', to five star hotels. A US cuppa consists of a tea bag attached to string presented on a saucer alongside a cup of lukewarm water. Once, at a golf club in Florida, a teapot was brought to the table. When the excitement had subsided we discovered that this just contained more warm water.

I once heard an American tour guide, I guess new to the job, rounding up her charges with the promise they were being taken to enjoy: 'A traditional beverage known as Devon Cream Tea.'

Cream Teas are the subject of inter-county controversy. A Cornish Cream Tea has the jam on the scone with the clotted cream on top. A Devon Cream Tea has the jam on top of the cream.

The first record I could find of what is now known as a Cream Tea comes from the twelfth century when builders at Tavistock Abbey were hit by a butter shortage so took to using clotted cream in its place.

End or dispute! The Cream Tea was invented in Devon, not Cornwall, and the cream goes on first.

In addition to giving birth to the Cream Tea, Tavistock also gave birth to Elizabethan naval hero Sir Francis Drake.

When our American tourists have got over the shock of steaming hot tea accompanied by one of the most delicious afternoon snacks known to mankind they will probably be taken to Plymouth where they congregate around two important tourist attractions.

At the top of Plymouth Hoe they will be shown the statue of Sir Francis Drake close to the spot where he finished a game of bowls before heading off to save England from the Spanish Armada.

It is doubtful Plymouth Hoe was ever smooth enough to play bowls, evidence suggests what is now the grassed area was once decorated with a hill carving of the giants Gog and Magogg. It is more likely that Drake was at an inn enjoying the local game of skittles.

Millions of Americans boast of being photographed next to the ancient statue of Sir Francis Drake on Plymouth Hoe. Sorry but that statue is just a copy of the original in Tavistock.

The second big attraction is the Mayflower Steps. (See Pilgrim Fathers)

French writer/philosopher Voltaire drank between 50 and 60 cups of tea every day.

TENNIS

Louis X and Charles VIII of France died of tennis related injuries.

The French Open takes its name from the Roland-Garros Stadium where it is staged. Roland Garros was a World War I pilot.

Yellow balls were introduced at Wimbledon in 1986 as they showed up on TV better than white ones.

Venus and Serena Williams were the first sisters to win Olympic gold medals for tennis. (See Olympics)

The first player to wear shorts at Wimbledon was Henry (Bunny) Austin in 1932.

The only major tennis tournament still played on grass is Wimbledon.

Boris Becker was the first German, the first unseeded player and the youngest player to win Wimbledon at the age of 17 in 1985.

During World War I the US Open was renamed the Patriotic Tournament.

The trophies for the Men's and Women's singles never leave Wimbledon. The winner's receive a small replica.

A very unscientific survey revealed that eight out of ten people think the Wimbledon Men's Singles Trophy is topped by a model of a tennis player, the other two had no idea. It is, in fact, topped by a pineapple. The pineapple represents the tradition of English sailors having a carving of a pineapple on their gateposts when they returned from a long voyage to celebrate fruit having warded off scurvy. (See Fruity)

The Wimbledon Women's Singles trophy is the Venus Rosewater Dish. Our ten-person sample were all wrong in their belief that the dish is named after a former winner.

A rosewater dish was used to catch scented water poured over diners' hands to clean them. The Wimbledon dish, made in Birmingham in 1864 at a cost of 50 guineas, is a copy of an antique in the Louvre, Paris. No matter what anyone at Wimbledon tells you the central figure is Sophrosyne, not Venus.

In 1896, John Pius Boland became the first to win an Olympic gold medal for tennis totally by accident. Boland was spending a vacation in Athens when the Olympics were taking place and one of his friends on the organising committee signed him up to play in the tennis tournament.

Boland won and then entered the doubles as a partner of Germany's Friedrich Traun, the guy he'd beaten in the first round of the singles, and they went on to win that.

THEFT AND THIEVES

Edward Jones was arrested four times for stealing Queen Victoria's underwear. (See Victoria)

Someone who compulsively steals women's underwear is a melcryptovestimentaphiliac.

THE HILLS ARE ALIVE

The 2015 Academy Awards celebrated the 50th anniversary of 'The Sound of Music' with Lady Gaga singing a medley of the film's songs at the end of which Julie Andrews walked on stage and embraced her.

'The Sound of Music' was Rodgers and Hammerstein's last musical. (See Award Ceremonies)

After the film's release in the mid 1960s Munich cinema goers were only shown the first two-thirds of 'The Sound of Music.' The movie ground to a halt shortly after the wedding scene, thus editing out Nazi attempts to prevent the Von Trapps' escape.

Maria von Trapp wasn't invited to the premier of 'The Sound of Music.'

In a 1962 Julie Andrew took part in a parody of the 'Sound of Music' at Carnegie Hall, titled, 'The Pratt Family Singers.'

Christopher Plummer, who played Captain von Trap, hated the movie so much he always referred to is as 'The Sound of Mucus.' He reportedly drank so much to drown his unhappiness during filming that his costumes had to be refitted because he put on weight.

Mia Farrow auditioned for Liesl before the role went to Charmain Carr.

During the filming of 'Sixteen Going on Seventeen', Charmain Carr fell through the glass in the gazebo. In the scene that made it to the screen she is wearing a bandage covered with make-up on her leg wounds. She was 22-years-old when she sang 'Sixteen Going on Seventeen.'

After their massive loss on 'Cleopatra', starring Elizabeth Taylor and Richard Burton, it was 'The Sound of Music' that saved 20th Century Fox.

In the movie the von Trapps escape over the mountains. In reality they caught a train to Italy. If they had hiked over the mountains they would have ended up in Germany close to Adolf Hitler's retreat. The day after the von Trapps escaped by train, Hitler ordered the German/Austrian border to be closed.

When the von Trapps moved out, their home was taken over by Heinrich Himmler. Hitler is known to have visited him there on several occasions. (See Hitler)

The 'Sound of Music' was so popular in South Korea that some cinemas showed it three or four times per day. One enterprising cinema manager increased the number of showings by clipping out all the musical numbers.

Despite Salzburg and other parts of Austria having a tourist industry virtually reliant on the film, 'The Sound of Music' is not well known in the country even though some hotels screen it in their rooms 24-7. In Austria the title of the film is 'Meine Leider - Meine Traume' ('My Songs - My Dreams') and the final scenes involving Nazis were cut before it was screened in the 1960s.

THUNDER AND LIGHTNING

Hats with lightning rods earthed to the ground by a trailing wire became fashionable in Europe after Benjamin Franklin published a design for making these.

At any given moment there are around 18,000 thunderstorms taking place on the Earth.

The average lightning bolt produces sufficient electricity to power a family home for a month.

Thunder is produced when lightning rapidly heats air causing it to expand and produce a sonic wave.

The average thunderstorm is 15 miles across and lasts for 30 minutes.

TIMELY

A 13-month calendar was used by the Kodak company from 1924 to 1989 and Kodak founder George Eastman campaigned for its international acceptance.

Americans refer to a very short period of time as a 'New York Minute.' It is claimed this term originated to describe the time between a traffic light turning green and the second car in line honking his horn.

Fortnight is used as the word for two weeks throughout Britain, Ireland and in many Commonwealth countries but in the USA and Canada most people refer to this period of time as biweekly.

Despite its massive size China has only one time zone. All clocks are set to Beijing Time.

TOURIST ATTRACTIONS

Marble Arch was designed in 1827 by John Nash as the State Entrance to Buckingham Palace. In 1851 it was relocated to its present position on a traffic island at the end of Oxford Street.

Historically the only people permitted to go through the Arch are members of the Royal Family and the King's Troop Royal Artillery.

I have lost count of the books and websites claiming Marble Arch was moved from its position at Buckingham Palace because the gold State Coach would not fit through it, however, during Victoria's coronation parade the gold State Coach passed through the Arch with room to spare. The relocation took place mainly because the Arch spoilt the view of the facade of the redesigned Buckingham Palace.

Buckingham Palace was built on the site of a notorious brothel.

Along with their entrance ticket, visitors to the Taj Mahal are handed a bottle of water and a pair of white cotton shoe covers. No drinks or snacks are sold, or even permitted, within the Taj. As you enter it is checked that your water bottle is still sealed so you cannot have replaced the contents with alcohol or a corrosive liquid, the water is your only drink during what is usually a long, hot tour. Indian people automatically remove their shoes and leave these at the bottom of the steps before going up to the iconic building which is set on a marble platform. So many Western tourists had problems with the concept of leaving their shoes unattended that they are provided with the covers so they can keep their shoes on.

The world's most popular tourist spot is the Las Vegas Strip with some 40 million visitors every year. New York's Times Square comes second with almost the same number of visitors. Surprisingly major tourist attractions outside the US come relatively low down on the popularity list: British Museum 40, Eiffel Tower 38, Great Wall of China 28, The Louvre 27.

In the 1950s tourists visited Las Vegas to view nearby atomic bomb tests. Las Vegas was marketed as 'Atomic City.'

The Great Pyramid at Giza, near Cairo, was constructed at about the same time the last wooly mammoth walked the Earth.

The three so-called Cleopatra's Needles in London, Paris and New York were made a thousand years before Cleopatra was born.

Until 1900 visitors to Stonehenge were loaned a chisel to chip off a souvenir.

The Eiffel Tower is six inches shorter in the winter than in the summer.

Writer Guy de Maupassant ate lunch each day beneath the Eiffel Tower because he said it was the only place in Paris where he didn't have to look at what he considered to be an extremely ugly structure.

Excited tourists visit Cawker City in Kansas to see the world's biggest ball of string.

Western visitors to the Great Wall of China, Terracotta Warriors and other tourist attractions in China are often surprised to find themselves to be of more interest to the local populace than the attraction they have come to see. Many Chinese people have never seen a Western face and will insist upon having selfies taken with you and you will be expected to hold their babies and pose with their children.

TURKEY

Turkeys were introduced to Britain in 1526 by William Strickland, a Yorkshireman. Strickland purchased six of the birds from American Indians and sold these for sixpence each in Bristol. (See Foreign Phrases)

Only male turkeys make the 'gobble gobble' sound, females click.

You don't need to invent an excuse to nap on Christmas day. It is a scientific fact that a turkey dinner makes you sleepy. This is due to the mix of carbohydrates that traditionally accompany the meat. Stuffing and potatoes alongside the turkey followed by a sugary dessert stimulate the release of insulin. This triggers most amino acids to flow from the blood into muscles. With the removal of other amino acids from the bloodstream, the remaining tryptophan has no competition and has an easy ride to the brain where it helps produce serotonin and this makes you sleepy.

It is a common fallacy that turkeys cannot fly. It is true that farmed turkeys can't get off the ground, usually due to excess weight and clipped wings. Wild turkeys can fly for short distances at speeds up to 55mph.

Turkeys prefer to sleep at the tops of trees.

A turkey has two stomachs. Food passes into the first stomach where it is broken down by gastric juices. From there it goes into the second stomach, or gizzard, which contains small stones and grit against which the food is ground into a mulch prior to passing back into stomach-number-one for further digestion.

It is possible for turkeys to reproduce without having sex.

Turkeys only whistle when they panic.

American Indians made arrowheads from the spurs on male turkey legs.

TV CHEFS

Philip Harben was the first chef to prepare a dish on British television. On July 12, 1946, at the height of wartime rationing, Harben treated the nation to his recipe for Lobster Vol-au-Vent.

While Jamie Oliver campaigns for kids to eat healthy food he seems to have little thought for how kids will be affected if they have to go through life with silly names. His four children are Buddy Bear Maurice, Poppy Honey Rosie, Petal Blossom Rainbow and Daisy Boo Pamela. If you think Gordon Ramsay uses bad language you want to find yourself stuck on a transatlantic flight within hearing range of Jamie Oliver!

After Jamie Oliver ($400 million) and Gordon Ramsay ($160 million) the world's third richest chef is listed as Wolfgang Puck ($90 million) and fourth Rachel Ray ($80 million). The latter two are virtually unknown outside the US. (Net worth of chefs estimated 2016)

TWINS

The scientific study of twins is gemellology.

Bloodhounds cannot detect the difference between the smell of identical twins.

Up to 22% of twins are left-handed as opposed to 10% of the non-twin population.

The average time between the birth of twins is 17 minutes.

William Shakespeare was the father of twins, a boy Hamnet and a girl Judith. (See Shakespeare)

The offspring of two sets of identical twins are genetically siblings but legally cousins.

If a mother is a fraternal twin the odds of her giving birth to twins increases four-fold.

25% of identical twins are mirror-image twins. Their hair falls in opposite directions, if one is right-handed the other is left-handed and they have mirror-image finger prints.

U

UNICORN

The modern conception of a unicorn is a sleek horse with a spiral horn growing upwards from the centre of its skull.

Unicorns were not always depicted in this image. Originally unicorns were pictured with the body of a horse, legs of a deer and the tail of a lion. The spiral horn projected forwards from the centre of the animal's forehead.

Unicorns are mentioned in the King James Version of the Bible but more modern versions change this to 'Wild ox.'

Mythological unicorns were said to be extremely ferocious. Only a virgin could capture a unicorn, once it was under her control it would meekly lie at her feet.

The single-horned unicorn is linked in many old books with early descriptions of a rhinoceros.

URBAN MYTHS
(or what Donald Trump would call Fake News)

It has become an established 'fact' that the English city of Birmingham has 22 more miles of canal than Venice.

While devising questions for Trivial Pursuit I was advised to include one invented and uncheckable fact in each edition to make it possible to monitor if people were stealing questions for their quiz books. (This was before the days when everyone checked everything on Google.)

I discovered that Birmingham does indeed have more miles of canal than Venice and turned this into the question: 'Which British city boasts 22 more miles of canals than Venice?' The actual mileage was my invention, 22 being the day of the month on which I was born.

This 22 miles has since been used as the answer to questions in books, on TV quiz shows, in rival trivia games and even in a tourist brochure for the city of Birmingham.

A Roll's-Royce broke down in Cairo and its owner telephoned the company to ask for the appropriate spare parts. An engineer was flown out from the UK to repair the car. When the owner finally arrived home he phoned Roll-Royce with his thanks and to enquire how much he owed them. He was told they had no record of what he was telling them as, 'Rolls-Royces don't break down.'

A motorist stopped to help fix someone's flat tyre. The stranded driver was so grateful he asked for his helper's address and several days later the motorist received $10,000 in the post from a grateful Donald Trump who he had not recognised.

J.F Kennedy visited Germany in the 1960s and during a speech he said, 'Ich bin ein Berliner' or, 'I am a Berliner.' While it is correct that there is a German donut called a Berliner, the people in the crowd understood perfectly what Kennedy was saying, did not think he was claiming to be a donut, and did not laugh him off stage as myth would have it.

It is not true that a tooth will dissolve if left in a glass of Coca-Cola.

None of the 'Star Trek' TV shows or movies include the phrase 'Beam Me Up Scotty.'

There is no truth in the myth that anyone wanting to work on an expedition in Antarctica must first have their wisdom teeth and appendix removed.

After his death Walt Disney was cryogenically frozen to be thawed and revived when cures become available for his various illnesses and old age. In some versions of this myth Disney's head was removed for preservation in liquid nitrogen. Disney was, in fact, cremated.

Shortly after 9/11 a photo circulated showing a tourist on a balcony at the top of one of the twin towers of the World Trade Centre with an aircraft approaching from behind about to smash into the building. The story claimed the camera was found several days after the disaster.

Although this image is still circulated on the internet, a Hungarian admitted to creating the image with Photoshop and apologised to families of victims for making light of their suffering.

Many Americans still believe the story that a town in Japan was re-named USA after World War II so it could legitimately export products with the label, 'Made in the USA.' (See Fads and Fashions)

There are no alligators in the sewers of New York that were purchased as pets, then, after outgrowing their aquariums in villas and apartments, were flushed down the loo.

In 1997 an email was circulated warning people to beware of strangers in bars. The story claimed that several people had been approached by a friendly businessman who plied them with drinks before driving them home. The drinks had been drugged and the victim wakes up in a bath of iced, bloody water some hours later to see a note telling him to urgently telephone for an ambulance. After seeking medical attention the poor guy discovers that his kidneys have been removed for sale on the black market.

Mama Cass died from choking on a ham sandwich despite the coroner's report that a heart attack killed her.

URINE

Ancient Romans imported urine from North Africa. It was used for tooth whitening by well-to-do ladies.

Prior to the discovery of yeast, urine was used to make bread rise.

Ancient Roman women drank poisonous turpentine claiming it made their urine smell like roses.

Fighter pilots wear a 'piddle pack' so they can urinate in flight.

Male and female astronauts pee into a funnel nicknamed 'Mr Thirsty'. This has a vacuum to suck urine into a container.

When the container is full the urine is jettisoned outside where it freezes into crystals.

It is claimed in an average year 225 Canadian men drown after falling overboard while urinating from the side of their fishing boats.

Cat urine glows under a UV black light.

Between eight and twenty teaspoonsful of urine are left behind in swimming pools for each swimmer.

The smelly urine that occurs after eating asparagus can be avoided by cutting off the tips but this defeats the whole point of eating asparagus as the tips are the best bits.

Children make invisible ink by writing with lemon juice which becomes visible when heated. Urine works just as well. (See Banks and Bankers)

Hippos urinate backwards.

You are always warned not to eat yellow snow, yellow snow melts more quickly than white snow because its darker colour absorbs more heat.

A male lobster's bladder is in its head. When lobsters fight they squirt their opponent's head with urine.

Chinook Indians enjoyed a delicacy known as 'Chinook Olives.' This was made by soaking acorns in urine for five months.

VALENTINES

Florists, chocolatiers and card shops enjoy their busiest time of the year, apart from Christmas, during the St Valentine's Day celebrations.

There were several Saint Valentine's but the most likely culprit for the annual love celebration is Saint Valentine of Terni, a third-century Saint who was martyred and buried at a cemetery in the north of Rome on 14th February AD 226.

Although still a Saint, in 1969 the Catholic Church decided so little was known about him, he might even have been two saints who'd become confused over the years, that they dropped him (or should that be them) from the General Roman Calendar permitting local churches to celebrate his day if and when they decided.

Before cards, chocolates and lashings of Prosecco became Valentine's Day essentials it was de rigueur to carry a flaming Cupid's Torch for your intended, hence 'carrying a torch.'

In Cuba February 14th is known as Loving Day. This is the most popular day of the year for weddings with the Palacios de los Matrimonios Social Club in Havana hosting as many as one hundred weddings on that single day.

VENICE

Venetian Blinds are known as Persian Blinds in Venice. They were invented in China.

Venice was once a country in its own right.

Images of the gondolier crooning romantic songs to his passengers was hit by complaints in the early 2000s from tourists who were transported along the Venetian canals by drunken gondoliers. In 2003 it became a major controversy in Venice when gondoliers were threatened with breathalyser and drugs tests. (See Urban Myths)

VICTORIA

Queen Victoria was only 4 feet 11 inches tall. She was always seated on a raised platform so she could be seen.

Victoria survived seven assassination attempts.

Victoria's first name was Alexandrina.

Prior to becoming Queen, Victoria was not allowed to walk up or down stairs unless someone was present to hold her hand. Her mother was extremely protective and even insisted that Victoria shared a bedroom with her.

Due to royal protocol Prince Albert was not allowed to propose to Victoria so she proposed to him.

Victoria publicly endorsed Vin Mariani, a cocaine-based drink that was a forerunner of Coca-Cola.

Victoria was buried with an item of Prince Albert's clothing and a plaster cast of his hand on her right side. On her left side, carefully concealed by a bouquet of flowers and wrapped in a silk handkerchief was a photograph of her beloved servant John Brown along with a lock of his hair.

VIRGIN QUEEN

Elizabeth I's cheeks became so sunken towards the end of her life, due to a combination of age and lack of teeth, that she never appeared in public without first padding out her face with silk handkerchiefs. History records it got to the point where Elizabeth had no teeth at all and the padding in her cheeks made it impossible to understand a word she said.

During her final years Elizabeth I was bald. (See Redheads)

It is said Elizabeth I only bathed once per month 'whether she needed it or not.' This quote came from a Venetian ambassador in a letter to his government. It has to be said that in Elizabethan times immersing oneself in water was said to be dangerous. It was thought the heat from the water opened your pours, permitting impurities and diseases in the water to flow into your body.

People said Elizabeth I was beautiful.

Elizabeth I established the office of Official Uncorker of Bottles making it compulsory that he alone must open any bottles found washed up on beaches in case important military information was enclosed within. (See Bottles)

Elizabeth I was the first owner of a wire coat hanger.

Elizabeth I outlawed wife beating after 10pm.

W

WARFARE

Indigestion salts were Britain's first anti-submarine deterrent. Barrel-loads of the salts were concealed on the seabed where remote controlled explosions were supposed to open the barrels as U-boats passed above. The salts were then expected to produce their familiar effervescence and float the U-boat to the surface and into the arms of the awaiting navy. The system was even less successful than bat bombs. (See Submarines) (See Batty)

The United Nations was originally established with the aim of winning World War II.

Britain was at war with Zanzibar for 38 minutes in 1896

The cost to the Allies of killing a single soldier in World War II was $22,500.

During the Siege of Jadotville (modern Likasi) in 1961, Irish troops were seriously outnumbered and eventually forced to surrender. Before giving up the fight they sent a radio message to HQ, 'We will hold out until our last bullet is spent. Could do with some whiskey.'

WARTS

Warthogs only have four warts. These are all on the head.

Despite being a common belief, it is a total myth that toads can cause warts.

Warts do not have roots. They grow on the surface of the skin.

Warts are contagious, they can be treated and they can be removed but they cannot be cured.

Huckleberry Finn's remedy for getting rid of warts was to swing a dead cat in a graveyard at night.

WATERFALLS

The Angel Falls in Venezuela is the world's highest uninterrupted waterfall. It has a height of 979 metres, more than three times the height of the Eiffel Tower. There are those who will tell you the Angel Falls took their name because when viewed from below they disappear into the heavens and are the tears of the angels. The falls actually take their name from the pilot Jimmy Angel who discovered them in 1935.

During a hot summer water from the Angel Falls turns to mist before it reaches the stream below.

Niagara Falls receive more visits from tourists than any other falls in the world due to their easy accessibility. The hotels around Niagara are a popular honeymoon destination and the falls are described as 'the second greatest disappointment in many marriages.'

Each year millions of Americans view the Niagara Falls from the US side of the border. Only 10% of the water flows over the American Falls and Bridal Veil on the US side, the other 90% flows down the main Horseshoe Falls in Canada.

Only 50% of the Niagara River makes it as far as the Falls, the rest is diverted for power. At night and during winter months this diversion is increased to 75%.

Robert Leach went over Niagara Fall in a barrel in 1911 and also became the first man to parachute into the Falls from a low-flying aircraft.

In 1926 Leach slipped on a fruit skin and died from complications that developed in the resulting broken leg.

Captain Webb, the first person recorded to have swum across the English Channel with no artificial aid, drowned in 1883 while trying to swim through the Whirlpool Rapids on the Niagara River. One of the most famous Englishmen of all time is buried at Oakwood Cemetery, Niagara Falls.

Spray from the Victoria Falls makes the Zambezi Rain Forest the only place on earth where it rains 24 hours a day, seven days a week, 365 days a year.

W.C.

In a former job I had to hire blocks of portable toilets for airshows and outdoor music events. The most aptly named company I found was 'W.C. In Fields'.

It is estimated that by peeing in the shower the average home can save 2,500 litres of water they would flush down the loo each year. (See Simpson Quotes)

Regulations require new public buildings in New York City to have twice as many toilets, or bathrooms as they are called in America, for women than for men.

'Anyone who hates children and dogs cannot be all bad.' — W.C. Fields

'If you can't baffle them with brains baffle them with bullshit.' — W.C. Fields

Women are like elephants. I like to look at them but I wouldn't want to own one. — W.C. Fields

WEDDINGS

When Princess Elizabeth, the future Queen Elizabeth II, married Lieutenant Philip Mountbatten, the future Prince Philip, Duke of Edinburgh, in 1947, their wedding presents included a shawl hand knitted by Mahatma Gandhi.

Prince Charles' wedding to Lady Diana was held at St Paul's Cathedral instead of the usual royal venue, Westminster Abbey. Although it was claimed this was because Charles wished to have less pomp and ceremony than an Abbey ceremony demanded. The real reason for the change of location was that 2,500 guests could be squeezed into St Paul's but only 1,800 into the Abbey.

A British old wive's tale claims bad weather on the wedding

day will result in a stormy marriage. A Hindu old wive's tale says rain on your wedding day brings good luck.

The accepted image of a groom walking his bride down the church aisle is celebrated in poem and song. The happy pair do not walk down the aisle. Church aisles are at the sides of the building, it's the nave that runs down the centre.

Brides in Britain are presented with a horseshoe because cold iron was supposed to drive away evil spirits.

Many countries maintain the tradition of throwing rice at the newly married couple rather than confetti. In Finland the number of grains of rice remaining stuck in the bride's hair signifies the number of children the duo will have.

The bride traditionally stands to the left of the groom during the ceremony because he needs his right hand free to hold his sword and fight off potential suitors.

'Mozart! He was happily married - but his wife wasn't.' — Victor Borge

An English tradition says a spider found within the folds of a wedding dress will bring good luck.

Wedding and engagement rings are worn on the fourth finger of the left hand because it was thought a vein ran from there direct to the heart.

Pearls are said to be bad luck in a wedding ring because their shape can represent a tear.

Until Queen Victoria started the custom for white wedding dresses brides simply wore their best clothes.

Cross-dressing was once popular with Danish brides and grooms to confuse evil spirits.

'I was married by a judge. I should have asked for a jury.' — Groucho Marx

Wedding cakes originated in ancient Roman times when guests and family broke a loaf of bread over the head of the bride to encourage fertility.

In Poland sugar was once sprinkled on the bride's bouquet to keep her sweet. (See Yuck!)

WELL SAID

'You don't have to eat the whole cow to know the meat is bad.' — Dr Johnson

'You should pick people for character. Intelligence you can always hire' — Henry Kissinger

WILL'S MOTHER

'All round Will's mother's' means a circuitous route. 'Black over

Will's mother's' means bad weather is on the horizon, usually coming from the East.

In some areas of the U.K. Will becomes Bill.

No amount of research has led to me discovering the identity of Will but some sources claim he is William Shakespeare whose mother lived in Stratford-upon-Avon and others name him as Kaiser Wilhelm II, the last Emperor of Germany and King of Prussia who abdicated at the end of World War One.

Why either of these would be referred to in this age-old phrase is not explained.

WINTER

Meteorologists define winter as the three coldest calendar months of the year. In the Northern Hemisphere this is December, January and February. In the Southern Hemisphere June, July and August.

It is a fact that more people suffer from colds and influenza during the winter but this is not because they are going out in inclement weather. Most winter illnesses are cause by staying indoors where viruses breed.

The Earth is closest to the Sun in December.

No Southern Hemisphere country has ever hosted, or even applied to host, the Winter Olympics. (See Olympics)

A scene in the movie 'Frozen' where two men argue over whether to stack firewood for the winter with the bark up or down was sparked by fact. Shortly before completion of the movie, TV in Finland aired what must have been a thrilling 12-hour programme about firewood in which two men had just this debate.

WORDS

The word 'trivia' derives from the Latin 'tri' + 'via', meaning three streets. At an intersection of three streets the ancient Romans often placed a small kiosk where information was posted. You might, or might not, be interested, hence 'trivia'.

The word 'agnostic' was coined by Aldous Huxley's grandfather Thomas Huxley.

'Polish' is the only word in the English dictionary that can be a verb or a noun and changes to a nationality when given an upper-case initial.

'Avocado' comes from the Spanish word 'aguacate' which is derived from 'ahuacatl' meaning 'testicle'.

'Uncopyrightable' is the only English word with 15 letters that can be spelled without repeating a letter.

'A rough-coated, dough-faced, thoughtful ploughman strode through the streets of Scarborough after falling into a slough he coughed and hiccoughed.' That sentence includes all nine different ways of pronouncing 'ough'.

'Latchstring' is the English word with the most consecutive consonants.

'Rhythm' and 'syzygy' are the longest English words without vowels.

The Scottish language is Gaelic. The Irish language is Gaeilge.

In her novel, 'Shirley', Charlotte Bronte makes the first known reference to the 'Wild West'.

Charlotte Bronte also coined the terms: 'Cottage-garden,' 'Raised eyebrow,' and 'Kitchen chair.'

'Dreamt' is the only English word ending in 'mt'.

WORKERS' RIGHTS

Darlington Council's 1983 audit revealed that £30,000 had been paid in overtime to crematorium workers for turning over a page in the Book of Remembrance before the doors were officially opened each morning.

A member of staff justified the payments by pointing out that the job wasn't the sort of thing that could be left to unskilled workers.

WRITERS' CRAMP

J. Rider Haggard originally wrote his classic novel, 'King Solomon's Mines,' with a full moon followed by a solar eclipse, followed by another full moon. When told that solar eclipses can only take place at new moon he changed the solar eclipses to lunar, thereby having three days of constant full moons.

Geoffrey Chaucer's most famous work is 'Canterbury Tales.' There is no evidence that Chaucer ever visited Canterbury.

There are more libraries in British prisons than in British schools.

Norwegian playwright Henrik Ibsen kept a live scorpion on his desk for inspiration.

Lord Byron made his half-sister pregnant.

Escapologist Harry Houdini bought Edgar Allan Poe's writing desk.

D.H. Lawrence claimed that climbing to the top of trees while naked brought him inspiration.

Whenever it looked as though a fight might break out in any of the rough bars they frequented, James Joyce would hide behind his much bigger buddy, Ernest Hemingway, and shout, 'Deal with him, Hemingway. Deal with him!'

Author Ray Bradbury's ancestor, Mary (née Perkins) Bradbury, was convicted and sentenced to hang as a witch at Salem in 1692. She evaded the sentence until the trials were discredited and died at the age of 85 in 1700.

J.R.R. Tolkien was rejected for a Nobel Literature Prize because of his 'poor storytelling.'

Dr Seuss pronounced his name Zoice.

Dr Seuss wrote 'Green Eggs and Ham' to win a bet with his publisher that he could write an entire book using only 50 different words.

X

XMAS

'Xmas at my house is always at least six or seven times more pleasant than anywhere else. We start drinking early and while everyone else is seeing one Santa Claus we'll be seeing six or seven.' — W.C. Fields (See W.C.)

I'm sure many people who have read this far will already be complaining about my spelling of Xmas. Xmas actually came before Christmas. X representing the Greek letter 'chi' which was commonly used and an abbreviation for the word 'Christ'.

The first Christmas postage stamp was issued by Austria in 1937.

If Santa travels at 650 miles per second he will have to visit around 50,000 homes every minute to make his deliveries.

Early Christmas celebrations included getting seriously drunk (not much changed there!), having sex and singing naked in the streets which was the origin of carol singing.

The original Christmas Pudding was a soup consisting of dried fruit in wine.

The word 'Noel' derives from the French 'les bonnes nouvelles' meaning 'The good news.'

y

YOU'RE FIRED

In 1986 I wrote a letter to the producers of long-running soap, 'Coronation Street', drawing their attention to an anomaly in the Street's layout. In their reply to my letter, they failed to admit it was my sharp-eyed observation that led them to burn down the Rovers Return then rebuild it with slightly more conventional architecture.

Ken Barlow, the Street's longest lasting resident, lived in a house previously occupied by his uncle, Albert Tatlock. When viewed from outside it was clear that this house shared a wall with the village pub. When the cameras went inside the Rovers the common wall was the one with the door to the toilets in it.

Or in other words, in the Old Rovers Return the ladies 'went' in Ken's lounge and at least the men had some form of plumbing because their loo was in Ken's kitchen.

This inconvenience could be why Ken was always so miserable.

In 2010 firefighters in Obion County, Tennessee let a house burn to the ground because the owner had not paid his annual $75 firefighting fee. The family lost all their possessions, three dogs and a cat. (See Great Fires)

YOU DIDN'T MEAN TO DO THAT

The composer Jean Baptiste Lulli died after gangrene set in to a wound inflicted when he stabbed his foot with his own baton.

The Just Missed it Club was formed for people who were due to sail on the Titanic but for some reason or other didn't. Two weeks after the Titanic sank the club had 118,337 members. (See Disasters)

YUCK!

Rhinotillexomania is the study of nose picking.

The record distance for projectile vomiting is 27 feet.

Brides originally carried flowers to mask their body odour. (See Weddings)

Dead people don't decompose as quickly as they once did due to preservatives in modern food.

The average kitchen sink harbours 100,000 times more germs than the average toilet bowl.

Z

ZODIAC

The Glastonbury Zodiac, also known as the Temple of the Stars, was discovered in 1935 by Katherine Maltwood. The theory is that a zodiac is depicted around the Glastonbury area, picked out by roads, streams, walls and canals. The circle of the Zodiac is eleven miles in diameter and the names of some locations within this are said to link with the Zodiac theory.

A phoenix outlined in the Zodiac rises from Cinnamon Lane, the legendary Phoenix arose from a fire made from cinnamon sticks. The breast of Virgo, the Virgin, is depicted by Toothill (Tit Hill).

There are several other Landscape Zodiacs around England, all with their supporters and their critics. Maps of and walking routes around the Glastonbury Zodiac are available online.

Interestingly I looked at maps of London, Paris and New York and it is possible to make out a very rude phrase from sections of the street patterns in these three cities so I'm sure, with a bit of imagination, you could create a zodiac just about anywhere.

ZYTHOLOGY

Zythology is the study of beer and brewing. (See Ale and Hearty)

Index

BLOOMING CRAZY

BOGEY

BOTTOMS

BRAS

BRIDGES

CAPITALS

CARLING

CARS

CELEBRITY SCENE

CENSORSHIP

CHARITABLE

CHEESE

CHILD BRIDES

CHINA

CHOCOLATE

CITY STATUS

CIVET

COLOURFUL

COMETS

COMPUTERS

CRITICS

CUSTOMS

DANCE

DANGEROUS STATISTICS

DATING

DEADLY

DESERTS

DING DONG

DISASTERS

DIVORCE

DOME SWEET DOME

DOVES OF PEACE (OR SHOULD THAT BE PIECES OF DOVE)

DRINK

eBAY

ECLIPTIC

EDUCATION

ELECTIONS

ELEMENTARY

ELVIS

ENGLISH IN OTHER LANGUAGES

EPITAPHS

EROS

ETIQUETTE

EXCLAMATION MARK!

EXECUTIONS

EXTRAS

FADS AND FASHIONS

FAILED ATTEMPTS

FASCINATING FACTS

FEET

FINAL THOUGHTS

FISHY FACTS

FLORAL TRIBUTES

FLYING HIGH

FOODY FADS

FOREIGN PHRASES

FRANCE

FRUITY

GAMESHOWS

GAS

GEORGE

GIMME SHELTER

GORGEOUS GIRLS

GRAFFITI

GREAT FIRES

HABITS

HALLOWE'EN

HAEMORRHOIDS

HAIR

HARRY POTTER

HEADLINE NEWS

HENRY VIII

HERBS AND SPICES

HIP-HIP-HOORAY

HITLER

HOGMANAY

HOMER SIMPSON - THE WIT AND WISDOM

HONEYMOONERS

HORSE RACING

HOT, HOT, HOT

HUMAN BODY

HUMP

IMMIGRATION

IMMORALITY

INFLATION

INSECTS

INSULTS

INVENTIONS

JAPAN

JAWS

JOINTS

KISMET

KUBLA KHAN

L.A.

LAKES

LAND'S END TO JOHN O'GROATS

LANGUAGE

LAW

LETTERS

LITTLE BASTARD

LITTLE LAMB

LOVE, LOVE, LOVE

LOVE TOKENS

MAD AS A HATTER

MAD KING

MAIL

MAN WHO BROKE THE BANK

MARCO POLO

MARGARETS

MASS HYSTERIA

MEASUREMENTS

MEN ON THE MOON

MICKEY MOUSE

MILK

MIRACLE

MIRROR IMAGE

MISTLETOE

MONEY, MONEY, MONEY

MUSIC

NAKED AS NATURE INTENDED

NAME CHANGE

NATIONAL COSTUME

NEWS

NIGHTINGALE

NOBEL

NOT AT ALL WELL

NUTS

NUTTING

ODD BODY PARTS

OH NO THEY DIDN'T

OH YES THEY DID

OKLAHOMA

OLYMPICS

OPIUM

ORGANS

OYSTERS

PACKAGE HOLIDAYS

PETOMANE

PETS

PILGRIM FATHERS

PIRATES

PLACE NAMES

PLAYTHINGS

POLLS

POLO

POO

POST MORTEM

PRESIDENTIAL

PUPPETS

QUOTABLE QUOTES

RAILWAYS

REDHEADS

REFERENCES

RELIGION

RIDER CLAUSES

RIVERS

ROADRUNNER

ROAD RUNNER

ROBIN HOOD

ROBOTS

ROCK ON

ROLLING STONES

ROYAL BOX

RULERS

SALT

SCAMS

SCHOOL

SCOTS

SERIAL KILLERS

SEVEN YEAR ITCH

SEXUAL EQUALITY

SHAKESPEARE

SHARING

SIMPSON QUOTES

SKIN

SING ALONG

SNOW

SOUVENIRS

SPACE PIONEERS

SPEED LIMITS

SPIDERS

SPORT

STRONG AND STABLE

SUBMARINES

SUN

SURREAL

TALE OF TWO ACCENTS

TATTOOS

TAXING

TEA TIME

TENNIS

THEFT AND THIEVES

THE HILLS ARE ALIVE

THUNDER AND LIGHTNING

TIMELY

TOURIST ATTRACTIONS

TURKEY

TV CHEFS

TWINS

UNICORN

URBAN MYTHS (OR WHAT DONALD TRUMP WOULD
CALL FALSE NEWS)

URINE

VALENTINES

VENICE

VICTORIA

VIRGIN QUEEN

WARFARE

WARTS

WATERFALLS

W.C.

WEDDINGS

WELL SAID

WILL'S MOTHER

WINTER

WORDS

WORKERS' RIGHTS

WRITERS' CRAMP

XMAS

YOU'RE FIRED

YOU DIDN'T MEAN TO DO THAT

YUCK!

ZODIAC

ZYTHOLOGY

By The Same Author...
IN PURSUIT
OF
TRIVIA

For 25 years Brian Highley wrote all of those questions for the many UK editions of Trivial Pursuit as well as TV quiz shows and satirical scripts for Spitting Image.

The question he is most often asked during TV and radio interviews is how he got the job writing for Trivial Pursuit. This memoir takes you through the life that perfectly fit him for the most trivial job on earth. There's nostalgia, there's humour and a few tears.

Along the way Brian gives Elton John his first major gig at a festival that left Elton a superstar and Brian a bankrupt. We rub shoulders with lots more rock stars, TV and movie celebrities, top politicians and even royalty.

Available on Amazon

BRIAN HIGHLEY

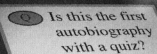

Q Is this the first
autobiography
with a quiz?

A Probably

IN PURSUIT
OF
TRIVIA

12357168R00162

Printed in Great Britain
by Amazon